Dear
Sophie,
Love
Sophie

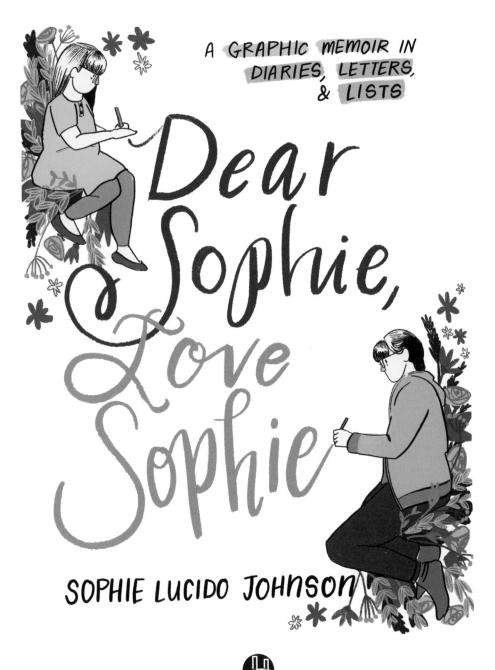

A GRAPHIC MEMOIR IN DIARIES, LETTERS, & LISTS

Dear Sophie, Love Sophie

SOPHIE LUCIDO JOHNSON

HarperOne
An Imprint of HarperCollinsPublishers

DEAR SOPHIE, LOVE SOPHIE. Copyright © 2022 by Sophie Lucido Johnson. All rights reserved. Printed in Thailand. No part of this book may be used or reproduced in any manner whatsoever without written permission except in the case of brief quotations embodied in critical articles and reviews. For information, address HarperCollins Publishers, 195 Broadway, New York, NY 10007.

Font copyright © Sophie Lucido Johnson.

HarperCollins books may be purchased for educational, business, or sales promotional use. For information, please email the Special Markets Department at SPsales@harpercollins.com.

FIRST EDITION

Library of Congress Cataloging-in-Publication Data has been applied for.

ISBN 978-0-06-304070-0

22 23 24 25 26   IMG   10 9 8 7 6 5 4 3 2 1

To my sister, Alexis.
You never tried to read my
diaries & I always tried
to read yours. I love you
unconditionally.

Prologue

DEAR READER,

LAST YEAR, I GOT THE WILDEST EMAIL. IT LANDED IN MY INBOX RIGHT BEFORE I WAS DUE TO RETURN TO MY ALMA MATER TO DO A BOOK READING, EXACTLY TEN YEARS AFTER I'D GRADUATED. THE EMAIL WAS FROM A CURRENT STUDENT AT THE COLLEGE, WHO LIVED IN THE HOUSE (DUBBED "THE WRITING HOUSE") WHERE I'D LIVED WHEN I WENT THERE. I WILL LET THIS EMAIL SPEAK FOR ITSELF:

Hello Sophie,

I am a student living at The Writing House this year and I believe we found something which belongs to you. Just a few days ago, my housemates and I were digging through a drawer and we found a journal which we believe to be yours. It is dated from August 2001 to February 2002, and refers to a sophomore in high school living in Portland whose name we believe to be Sophie, though she signs as S. If this is not you, I apologize for bothering. If it is your journal, on behalf of The Writing House, I have a request. We were wondering if you would be willing to participate in an event either before or after your already scheduled event on Thursday the 20th. We are willing to let you decide what you want to do with the event but we were hoping you could: read or discuss your journal, talk about how writing in your journal helped to develop your voice or writing style, talk about the process of publishing a book, answer some questions regarding what happened to Eli and/or Trevor.

Thank you for your consideration.

Admirably,

Cam

INDEED, THIS <u>WAS</u> MY JOURNAL (WELL, IT WAS MY DIARY, BUT SAME DIFFERENCE), AND I'D HAD NO IDEA IT WAS EVEN <u>MISSING</u>. I'M A LIFELONG DIARIST, AND I KEEP MY JOURNALS WELL ORGANIZED, SO IT WAS WILD TO ME THAT SOMEONE HAD FOUND IT AND HAD MANAGED TO TRACK ME DOWN; I WAS EVEN MORE FLOORED THAT I WOULD BE IN TOWN THAT WEEKEND AND WOULD HAVE A CHANCE TO MEET THE PERSON WHO HAD DISCOVERED MY DIARY.

I WENT TO WALLA WALLA, I MET CAM, AND I READ OUT LOUD FROM MY DIARY — YOUNG SOPHIE'S DIARY — IN FRONT OF A NUMBER OF PEOPLE SO UNEXPECTEDLY LARGE THAT THEY COULD BARELY ALL FIT IN THE HOUSE. THERE'S SOMETHING INTRIGUING ABOUT SOMEONE ELSE'S DIARY, I GUESS. THE EVENT WAS INTENDED TO LAST AN HOUR, BUT IT WENT MUCH LONGER; THERE WAS A <u>LOT</u> OF LAUGHING. BUT IT DIDN'T FEEL AS IF YOUNG SOPHIE WAS BEING LAUGHED AT; IT FELT AS IF SHE WAS BEING APPRECIATED FOR THE FUNNY, STRANGE,

UNIQUE YOUNG PERSON SHE'D WANTED TO BE (AND
BE SEEN AS). AFTER I FINISHED THE READING, A
GIRL CAME UP TO ME. "I KNOW YOU'RE OLDER, BUT I
STILL FEEL LIKE THERE WAS SO MUCH OF ME WHEN
I WAS YOUNGER IN THAT DIARY," SHE SAID. "I WISH
YOU COULD HAVE READ THE WHOLE THING TO US."

EVERY DAY OR SO, SINCE I WAS OLD ENOUGH TO
WRITE, I'VE GOTTEN UNDER THE COVERS OF MY BED
WITH A SHARP PENCIL OR, LATER, A COOL GEL PEN,

AND POURED OUT THE FACTS AND EMOTIONS OF THE DAY. WHEN I LOOK BACK AT THE EARLY ENTRIES NOW, I'M TRANSPORTED. ALL OVER AGAIN I REMEMBER WHAT IT FELT LIKE FOR TREVOR HANCEY NOT TO LOVE ME BACK; FOR ALL MY FRIENDS TO HAVE GONE TO A BIRTHDAY PARTY WITHOUT ME; TO BE FAILING A CLASS I SHOULD HAVE BEEN ACING. BEING YOUNG IS TERRIBLE. YOU HAVE NO UNDERSTANDING OF YOUR OWN APTITUDE TO GET THROUGH ANYTHING YET.

A FEW YEARS AGO, I STARTED WRITING LETTERS BACK TO MY CHILDHOOD SELF. I NAMED

THIS PROJECT "DEAR SOPHIE, LOVE SOPHIE." I SOMETIMES PUT THESE LETTERS UP ON MY BLOG, AND I SOMETIMES KEPT THEM FOR MYSELF. MY THIRTY-FIVE-YEAR-OLD CURRENT SELF LIKES TO IMAGINE THAT THERE'S AN

OLDER VERSION OF <u>HER</u> SOMEWHERE IN THE FUTURE WHO WILL KNOW WHAT TO DO ABOUT THE BIG TOPICS OF THE MOMENT, AND THAT SOMEDAY, THESE PROBLEMS WILL ALL FEEL UTTERLY FAR AWAY.

I'VE BEEN SPENDING A LOT OF TIME WITH YOUNG SOPHIE, TRYING TO SEE IF SHE HAS SOMETHING TO TEACH ME ABOUT MYSELF. YOUNG SOPHIE ISN'T THE BEST PEN PAL, BUT SHE IS IN A WHOLE OTHER TIMESCAPE, AND THE PRICE OF POSTAGE BETWEEN TIMESCAPES IS SUPER HIGH. IF SHE WON'T WRITE ME BACK, AT LEAST I CAN SHARE THESE CORRESPONDENCES WITH YOU. SINCE I WROTE IN MY DIARY BASICALLY EVERY DAY IN MY YOUTH, AND SOMETIMES TWICE A DAY, I'VE SPARED YOU A LOT OF ENTRIES. THE OMITTED ONES ARE MOSTLY ALL ABOUT SUMMER CAMP FOOD, WHETHER I SHOULD GROW OUT MY BANGS, AND BAD MUSIC FROM THE EARLY AUGHTS THAT I'M EMBARRASSED ABOUT. YOU DON'T NEED THAT.

I'VE SORTED SOME OF THE MOST INTERESTING
ENTRIES INTO CATEGORIES, AND I PRESENT THEM TO
YOU THEMATICALLY RATHER THAN CHRONOLOGICALLY.
SINCE THIS IS SOMETIMES CONFUSING (SORRY! I
PICKED "CONFUSING" OVER "BORING"), I'VE INCLUDED
SOME PAGES WITH CONTEXT. THOSE PAGES HAVE
YELLOW BOXES, AND THEY SHOULD HELP PLACE
YOU IN TIME. I WANTED TO EXPLORE TOPICS LIKE
BODY IMAGE, RELATIONSHIPS, SEXUAL IDENTITY,
OUR SENSE OF BELONGING AND IDENTITY—
UNIVERSAL ISSUES THAT MOST OF US DEAL WITH AT
SOME POINT IN OUR LIVES. AS I JOURNEYED

THROUGH THE OLD DIARIES, I WAS INTERESTED TO SEE THE SPECIFIC THINGS I DEALT WITH AS A FOURTEEN-YEAR-OLD, BOTH THE ONES I'VE GROWN PAST AND THE ONES I'M STILL DEALING WITH. I CAME TO THIS PROJECT THINKING THAT I WOULD HAVE A LOT TO TEACH YOUNG SOPHIE, BUT IT TURNS OUT, SHE HAS PLENTY TO TEACH ME AS WELL.

MY HOPE IS THAT THIS EXPERIMENT OFFERS YOU A
CHANCE TO REFLECT ON WHO YOU ARE—AND WHO
YOU WERE. WHAT YOUR DREAMS WERE, WHO YOU
THOUGHT YOU'D BE, THE HUMANS YOU KISSED (OR
DIDN'T), THE TEARS YOU CRIED (OR STOICALLY
HELD BACK), THE DEMONS THAT MIGHT NOT HAVE
LEFT YOU YET. THAT LAST ONE, I BELIEVE, IS OF
CRITICAL IMPORTANCE.

BRAIN RESEARCH IS WITH ME ON THIS: THE STUFF
THAT HAPPENED TO YOU WHEN YOU WERE A KID
IS ALMOST DEFINITELY STILL WITH YOU. IF YOU
EXPERIENCED TRAUMA, THERE'S A WHOLE
SECTION OF YOUR BRAIN COMMITTED TO WORKING
THROUGH THAT TRAUMA. THAT PART OF YOUR
BRAIN (THE HIPPOCAMPUS) GOES CRAZY WHEN
IT'S TRIGGERED BY SOMETHING THAT REMINDS
YOU OF THE PAIN FROM YOUR PAST. YOUR BRAIN
WANTS TO HELP YOU HEAL, BUT IT NEEDS TIME
AND DEDICATED SPACE. THE HEALING PROCESS
REQUIRES NOT ONLY AN ACQUAINTANCE WITH YOUR

YOUNGER SELF, BUT PATIENCE AND LOVE FOR THAT
SELF, TOO.

WE DON'T NEED A WORLD FULL OF PEOPLE WHO
ARE TOUGH. WE NEED A WORLD FULL OF PEOPLE
WHO ARE KIND. AND WE NEED A WORLD FULL OF
PEOPLE WHO UNDERSTAND THEMSELVES ENOUGH TO
RESPOND TO THEIR OWN TRAUMA WITH PATIENCE,
SLOWNESS, FULLNESS, AND HUMOR. THIS IS WHAT
MAKES HUMANS RESILIENT. IT IS HOW WE CREATE A
BETTER SPECIES. IT IS HOW WE EVOLVE.

THE PARTS OF YOUNG SOPHIE THAT GOT HURT ARE
ACHING TO BE SEEN, HELD, AND HEALED. SPENDING
TIME WITH THIS OLD ACHE CREATES SPACE FOR THE
PERSON I'M GROWING INTO NOW. I HOPE FUTURE
SOPHIE IS GRATEFUL FOR THIS WORK. BUT I THINK
THIS IS BIGGER THAN ALL THE SOPHIES PUT
TOGETHER. I DON'T THINK WE'RE GIVEN ENOUGH
ROOM, CULTURALLY, TO FEEL BIG FEELINGS WHEN
WE'RE YOUNG — AND WHEN WE'RE YOUNG IS WHEN

WE'RE <u>SUPPOSED</u> TO BE FEELING THEM. INSTEAD,
WE'RE PRESSURED TO SMASH EVERYTHING DOWN
AND MOVE ON, ALL WHILE OUR LITTLE BRAINS ARE
STILL DEVELOPING. THEN OUR GROWN-UP SELVES
HURT THE <u>NEXT</u> GENERATION OF CHILDREN, BECAUSE

WE THINK THAT'S HOW
IT HAS TO BE DONE;
THAT'S HOW WE GET
TOUGH.

WHILE I'M TALKING
BRAIN SCIENCE AND
TRAUMA HEALING
HERE, I URGE YOU
TO ALSO BUY AND
DEVOUR THE BOOK
<u>MY GRANDMOTHER'S HANDS</u>, BY RESMAA MENAKEM.
I KNOW, I KNOW: I HAVEN'T EVEN STARTED IN ON MY
OWN THING YET AND ALREADY I'VE CREATED A
LITANY OF STUFF FOR YOU TO READ AND TO DO.
SORRY NOT SORRY, FRIENDS.

WHAT EXACTLY IS IT THAT I'M ASKING YOU TO <u>DO</u>?
I'M ASKING YOU TO PAY ATTENTION TO THE PERSON
YOU WERE, AND SEE IF THERE ARE THINGS YOU
STILL HAVE TO WORK THROUGH. MAYBE YOU HAVE
A DIARY YOU CAN READ AND WRITE BACK TO. MAYBE
YOU HAVE A SIBLING YOU CAN SIT DOWN AND TALK
WITH. NO MATTER HOW YOU DO IT, I'M ASKING YOU
TO MAKE SOME SPACE AND TIME FOR YOUNG YOU,
AND TO SEE WHAT COMES UP. THE STAKES ARE
HIGH. THIS IS THE WORK WE ALL NEED TO DO TO
MAKE THE WORLD BETTER THAN IT IS NOW FOR
THE HUMANS WHO COME NEXT. SOULS IN PAIN
HAVE TO WORK FIVE TIMES AS HARD (AT LEAST)
TO GET GOOD WORK DONE. AND WE SHOULD ALL
BE ABLE TO AGREE THAT THERE IS GOOD WORK
TO BE DONE.

NAMES HAVE BEEN CHANGED IN THIS BOOK,
BECAUSE A LOT OF THIS INFO IS TOP SECRET, AS
YOU'LL SOON REALIZE. I APPRECIATE THE PEOPLE
WHO LOANED ME THEIR LIKENESSES, EVEN THOUGH

I DIDN'T ALWAYS HAVE THE OPPORTUNITY TO ASK
THEM IF IT WAS OKAY. THANK YOU, PEOPLE!

AND FINALLY, THANK <u>YOU</u>, READER. LATELY I'VE
BEEN FEELING LIKE BOOKS ARE THINGS YOU CAN
INTERACT WITH; THEY'RE COLLABORATIONS BETWEEN
READERS AND WRITERS. SO PLEASE FEEL FREE TO
WRITE ME BACK! I'M A <u>GREAT</u> PEN PAL, AND I DON'T
THINK WE'LL HAVE TO DEAL WITH THAT QUANTUM
TIMESCAPE POSTAGE.

LOVE,
SOPHIE

Chapter
ONE:
Young Sophie,
MEET
Today Sophie

THESE ENTRIES TAKE PLACE BETWEEN THE YEARS 1999 AND 2004.
BECAUSE THEY'RE ORGANIZED BY THEME, THEY'RE NOT TOTALLY CHRONOLOGICAL.
FEEL FREE TO REFER BACK TO THESE PAGES TO UNDERSTAND THE SUBTLE
BUT SIGNIFICANT CHANGES IN OUR HERO, YOUNG SOPHIE.

YEAR: 1999/2000

AGE: 14

GRADE: 9

LOVE INTERESTS:
MANY & FLUCTUATING,
BUT THE MAJOR
CHARACTERS ARE JOE
& TREVOR.

FRIENDS: BASICALLY, JOE &
TREVOR. SOPHIE & JOE HAVE
BEEN FRIENDS SINCE THEY
WERE FIVE.

FAMILY: MOM & DAD ARE
MARRIED & WORK AT A COLLEGE.
SISTER ALEXIS IS TWO YEARS
YOUNGER.

INTERESTS: FRANCESCA LIA BLOCK
BOOKS, RIDER STRONG FROM
BOY MEETS WORLD, GROWING
LONGER HAIR, THE SPICE GIRLS
(BUT NOT OPENLY), SCRUNCHIES,
VEGETARIANISM, POETRY.

DISLIKES: PASTA, MOST OF
THE GIRLS AT SCHOOL,
ALL SCIENCE CLASSES,
SPORTS, DAWSON'S CREEK,
OUTSIDE.

YEAR: 2001

AGE: 15

GRADE: 10

LOVE INTERESTS: TREVOR. TREVOR ALL DAY ALL NIGHT. TREVOR FOREVER.

FRIENDS: GIRLS! JESSICA, ZOE, KELLIE, & SHEILA. AND THEIR BOYFRIENDS.

INTERESTS: SONGWRITING, NO DOUBT, MANIC PANIC HAIR DYE, ENVIRONMENTALISM, JOINING LOTS OF CLUBS.

DISLIKES: JEANS, ROPE CLIMB IN GYM CLASS, MOST CARTOONS, SALAD DRESSING, VIDEO GAMES.

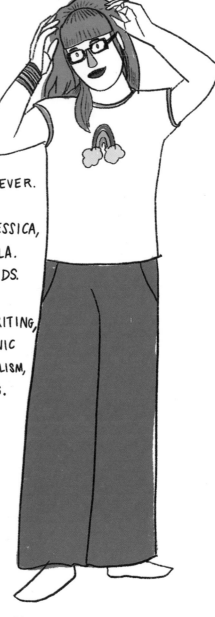

YEAR: 2002

AGE: 16

GRADE: 11

LOVE INTERESTS: ELI.

FRIENDS: THERE ARE
LOTS! MAYBE THERE
ARE TOO MANY TO LIST.
BUT JESSICA & BEN ARE
THE MAIN ONES.

INTERESTS: SOCIAL JUSTICE,
THE ACTOR CILLIAN MURPHY,
VEGANISM, BEN FOLDS.

DISLIKES: GEORGE W.
BUSH, FUNDAMENTALIST
CHRISTIANITY, THE DENTIST,
GAP CLOTHING,
AVRIL LAVIGNE.

YEAR: 2003

AGE: 17

GRADE: 12

LOVE INTERESTS: BEN.

FRIENDS: MOSTLY JUST BEN.

INTERESTS: R-RATED MOVIES, ACTIVISM IN ALL ITS MANY FORMS, THE UNITARIAN CHURCH, EMO MUSIC, AVRIL LAVIGNE (BUT IRONICALLY).

DISLIKES: ALCOHOLISM, SCARY MOVIES & TV, CHOCOLATE, PSYCHOTHERAPY, MOST GIRLS.

1/3/2000

Dear Diary,

High school is a sort of traumatizing time. And I kept telling myself Joe wouldn't want to stand by me through all that is hard and challenging, but deep in my heart, I thought that he would. He's JOE. He's the person I tell everything to, somewhere inside I just thought, well, I don't know, that he'd take my hand and rough it with me — but he hasn't. And that disappoints me. But... if I finish the entry this way, I'll go to sleep in tears, so I'm going to to have to make myself feel better somehow.

I'll shower myself with compliments. I am beautiful, inside and out. I am kind, compassionate, and funny. I'm a little melodramatic, but that's ok. I'm talented. I am entirely blessed. My mother loves me, my father loves me, my sister loves me. My life is wonderful. I have two great cats, a dog, and three adorable hamsters. My life is one that lots of people care about and cherish. People clap when I read my poetry out loud. I have been in love, and I can run a mile. I can make new friends. My life amounts to a lot, several people envy me. I'm sexy, talented, and smart. I can write music, and draw, and people admire my style.

Why don't I feel better?

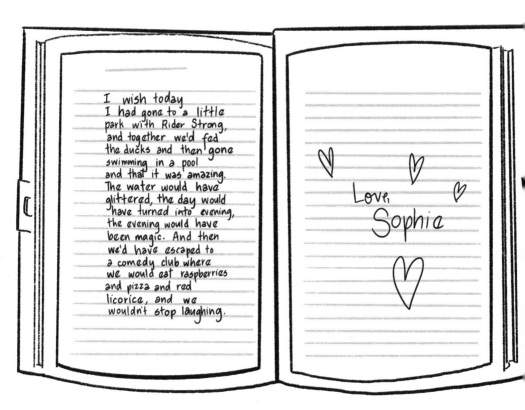

I wish today
I had gone to a little
park with Rider Strong,
and together we'd fed
the ducks and then gone
swimming in a pool
and that it was amazing.
The water would have
glittered, the day would
have turned into evening,
the evening would have
been magic. And then
we'd have escaped to
a comedy club where
we would eat raspberries
and pizza and red
licorice, and we
wouldn't stop laughing.

Love,
Sophia

Dear Sophie,

Girl: high school was <u>incredibly</u> traumatic. I can 100 percent validate that. As an adult, I have learned that actually

WE DON'T HAVE TO FIX EVERYTHING ALL THE TIME.

All that is usually necessary is a little validation.

My husband taught me that.

My husband whose name is <u>not</u> Joe.

But I also appreciate how you took on the herculean task of making yourself feel better, no matter the results.

Your compliment stream reads a little like a gratitude list. In my journals now, I write a gratitude list at the bottom because

FEELING GRATEFUL CAN CHANGE YOUR WHOLE DAY.*

*SCIENCE SAYS →

Although, I'll confess I try to be quirkier than listing my family members & cats. I try to include things like (& THIS IS AN EXACT QUOTE):

GRATITUDE.

① Today I thought I saw a cockroach, but it turned out to only be an old leaf.

I look back at you & see a girl who is all the things you wrote in your entry (except maybe the part about being sexy, because you're fourteen), <u>PLUS</u> terrified & sad & confused.

Those three latter things seem bad, but they aren't. Uncomfortable feelings aren't bad; they're human.

It is okay to feel them.

The raspberries & red licorice with Rider Strong thing still sounds very cool to me. Very, very cool. & I'm going to hold out that such a reality could someday still come true. Let's check in with Future Sophie in twenty more years, okay? Maybe she'll have some good news.

Love, Sophie

Here's me now.

YEAR: 2022

AGE: 35

OCCUPATION(S):
HIGH SCHOOL &
COLLEGE TEACHER &
CARTOONIST. WOW!

INTERESTS:
BIRDS, OUTSIDE,
BREAD BAKING,
SUMMER, PLAYING
ACCORDION, D&D,
MY CATS, COMIX.

DISLIKES:
XENOPHOBIA,
BIGOTRY,
SUVS,
MEAT,
THE FONT PAPYRUS,
ULTRAVIOLENT MOVIES.

This is my yellow house! I own it!

LOVE INTERESTS:
LUKE & BOB & KAT.
← (& Luke even married me!)

LOCATION:
CHICAGO

Chapter
Two:

I Want Nothing
More Than
A Boyfriend

10/24/2000

Dear Diary,

Don't tell anyone 'cause I
play out the opposite: I
want nothing more than a boyfriend. I won't tell anyone.
No one. I want to tell people,
but I really hate to be too
selfish, but oh GOSH my
hormones are in full blast, and
I just need some arms to fall
into. I'm a little afraid, you
know? A bit scared to go into
anything for fear that it will
be out of pity. Because, let's
face it: no one wants to date
a fat, ugly, extremely out-
landish fourteen-year-old. I am
fixed that there is someone
out there who is perfect for
me but I wish he'd
find me already and get done

with it 'cause I'm tired of
waiting.

God, what a DEMON I am.
I'm lucky! Oh lord, if you
read diaries, forgive me.
Don't waste your power on
me. Stop world hunger
instead. Or at least make
Samantha Ingles happy.
She seems truly depressed.

Love,

Sophie

Dear Sophie,

Here is a major spoiler: you're going to date SO MANY PEOPLE.

You are literally going to write a whole book about all the people you dated.

(OH YEAH! I PUBLISHED A BOOK! THANK YOU, YES, I AGREE, IT'S IMPRESSIVE.)

That book will contain an actual timeline of boyfriends so that your readers can keep track of all the many, many boyfriends you are going to have.

But I'm not sure that telling you this is going to make you calm down about wanting a boyfriend.

Let me just say:
YOU'RE NOT A DEMON,
&
I AM PRETTY SURE GOD DOESN'T READ DIARIES.

(It would be beneath her, I think, although there's no real telling when it comes to God.

I don't even know if God is her name!

It is possible that when we say "God" we mean "Quantum Physics" or "Nature" or "Beyoncé" [just wait]. Anyway, I'm not sure how we started talking so much about God. We were talking about boys.)

Love,
Sophie

1993:

OH THANK GOD YOU'RE HERE, TREVOR. CAN YOU PLEASE FIX THE VCR?

No PROBLEM.

"click"

THAT SHOULD DO IT!

1997:

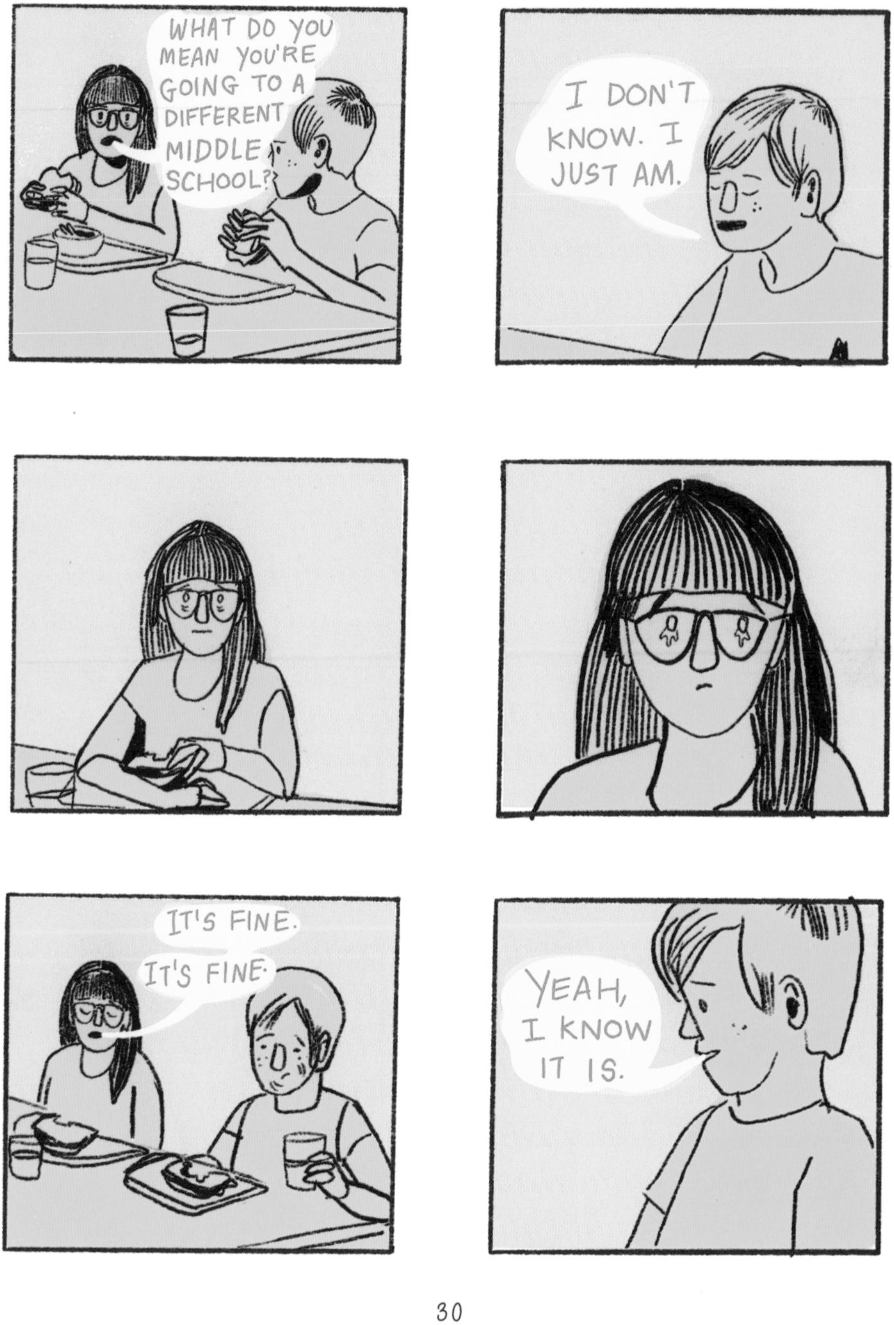
WHAT DO YOU MEAN YOU'RE GOING TO A DIFFERENT MIDDLE SCHOOL?
I DON'T KNOW. I JUST AM.
IT'S FINE.
IT'S FINE.
YEAH, I KNOW IT IS.

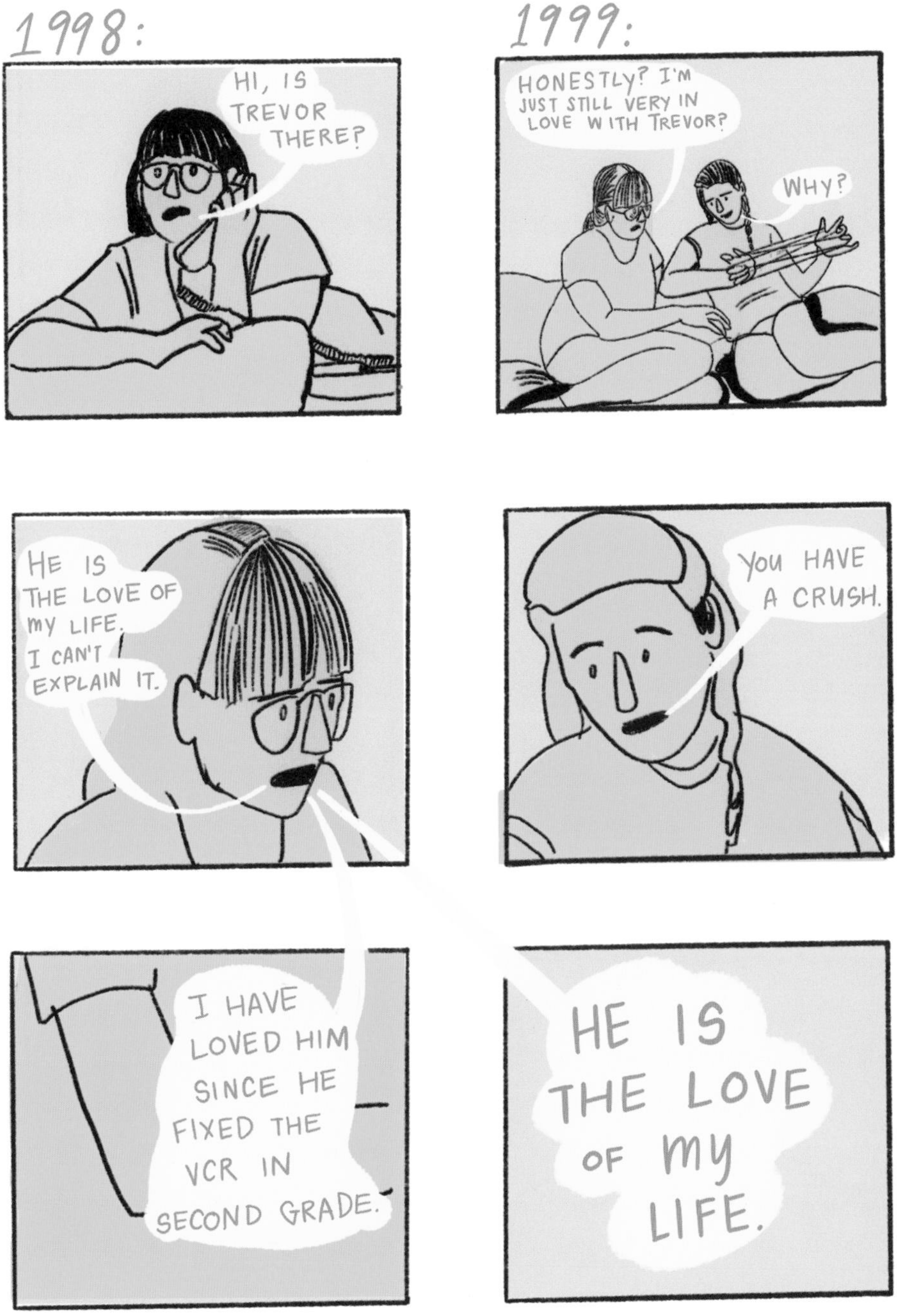
1998:
HI, IS TREVOR THERE?
1999:
HONESTLY? I'M JUST STILL VERY IN LOVE WITH TREVOR?
WHY?
HE IS THE LOVE OF MY LIFE. I CAN'T EXPLAIN IT.
YOU HAVE A CRUSH.
I HAVE LOVED HIM SINCE HE FIXED THE VCR IN SECOND GRADE.
HE IS THE LOVE OF MY LIFE.

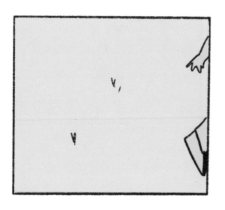

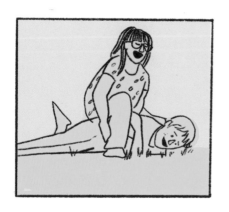

2000:

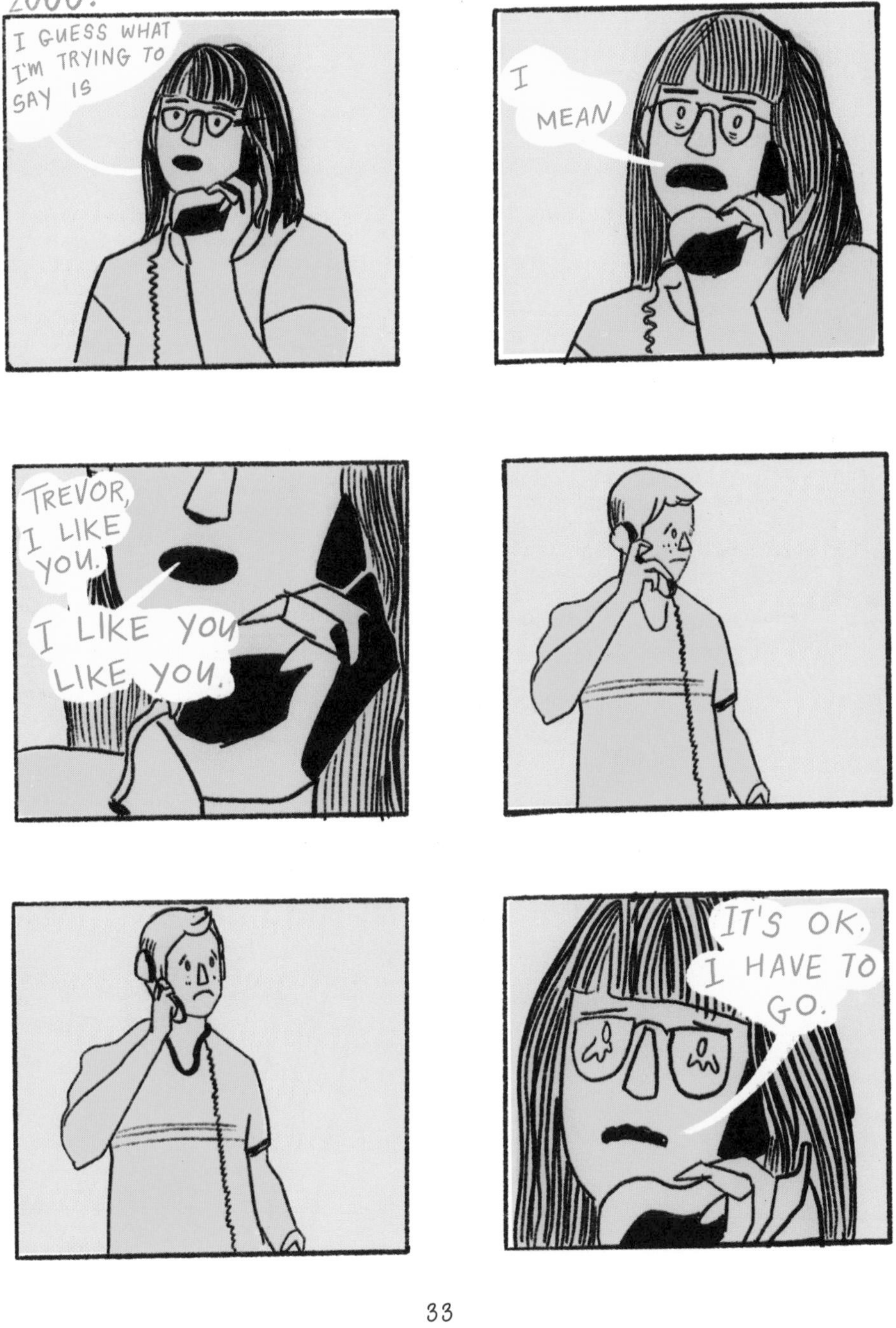
I GUESS WHAT I'M TRYING TO SAY IS
I MEAN
TREVOR, I LIKE YOU.
I LIKE YOU LIKE YOU.
IT'S OK. I HAVE TO GO.

8/28/2001

Dear Diary,

I have made a decision. I no longer am in love with Trevor. I know this is rather rash of me and unexpected. But I have decided to move on. For scientific purposes, of course, I am still allowed to daydream about him. BECAUSE I HAVE TO DO THAT TO SURVIVE. But I have to stop being obsessed over the guy. He isn't THAT great. Maybe he's NOT the love of my life. Maybe he's just another guy that I've met and another guy I never had much of a chance with, but I kept trying to tell myself I did. Because I'm so weird and I think all guys COULD

like me, maybe, if they wanted to. Yeah, right. The sad truth of the matter is that I'm simply a repulsive human being, and men don't love me. That's an understatement. No one of any gender could love me. That isn't such a depressing thing, in the scheme of things. I mean, apparently, I'll someday grow a set of breasts. That'll be the day, huh? Perhaps one day I'll even grow out of this awkward fat phase, and I MIGHT EVEN GROW INTO MY NOSE. But not for a while. For now, I'm living in Eternal Singlesville. I mean, it's a nice place to live, really. So, maybe nothing will ever happen with Trevor.

I will always love Trevor.

But GOOD GOD I need to get a life.

Move on!

That ship has sailed.

Goodbye, Ship!

I will miss you.

Love, Sophie

8/29/2001

Dear Diary,

Ugh. I'm in a rut. I think I'm just tired of being me (whine whine whine, blah blah blah). Maybe it's 'cause I'm not in love with Trevor. And I'm really not in love with him, believe me! No, seriously. Don't you believe me? Does it mean anything that just thinking about calling him made my heart beat so loud that one could un—doubtedly hear it in China? Does it matter that I did call him and he wasn't home and I left a message and now whenever the phone rings I leap up to get it with a wild spring? Noooooooo. That matters NOT. It is obvious that I am extremely over him.

Extremely so.

Radically so.

Recklessly so.

I'm a damned walking thesaurus over him, because my mind is clear of all thoughts about stupid individuals named Trevor. And so now I can think about synonyms in depth because of my clear mind.

(The phone rang. I jumped wildly. It was Tracy with Country Insurance, not Trevor.)

Love,
Sophie

Dear Sophie,

You spent a lot of time & energy wondering why Trevor didn't love you (& trying to convince yourself not to love Trevor), WHICH I GET. So I am very excited to tell you that, in 2018, I finally had the opportunity & courage to ask Trevor about all of this.

After I published my book, I went to Portland (I no longer live there) to do a reading at Powell's. (POWELL'S! OUR FAVORITE PLACE ON EARTH! I KNOW!). I was one sentence in when—

Oh my GOD! Wait, is that— TREVOR H.?

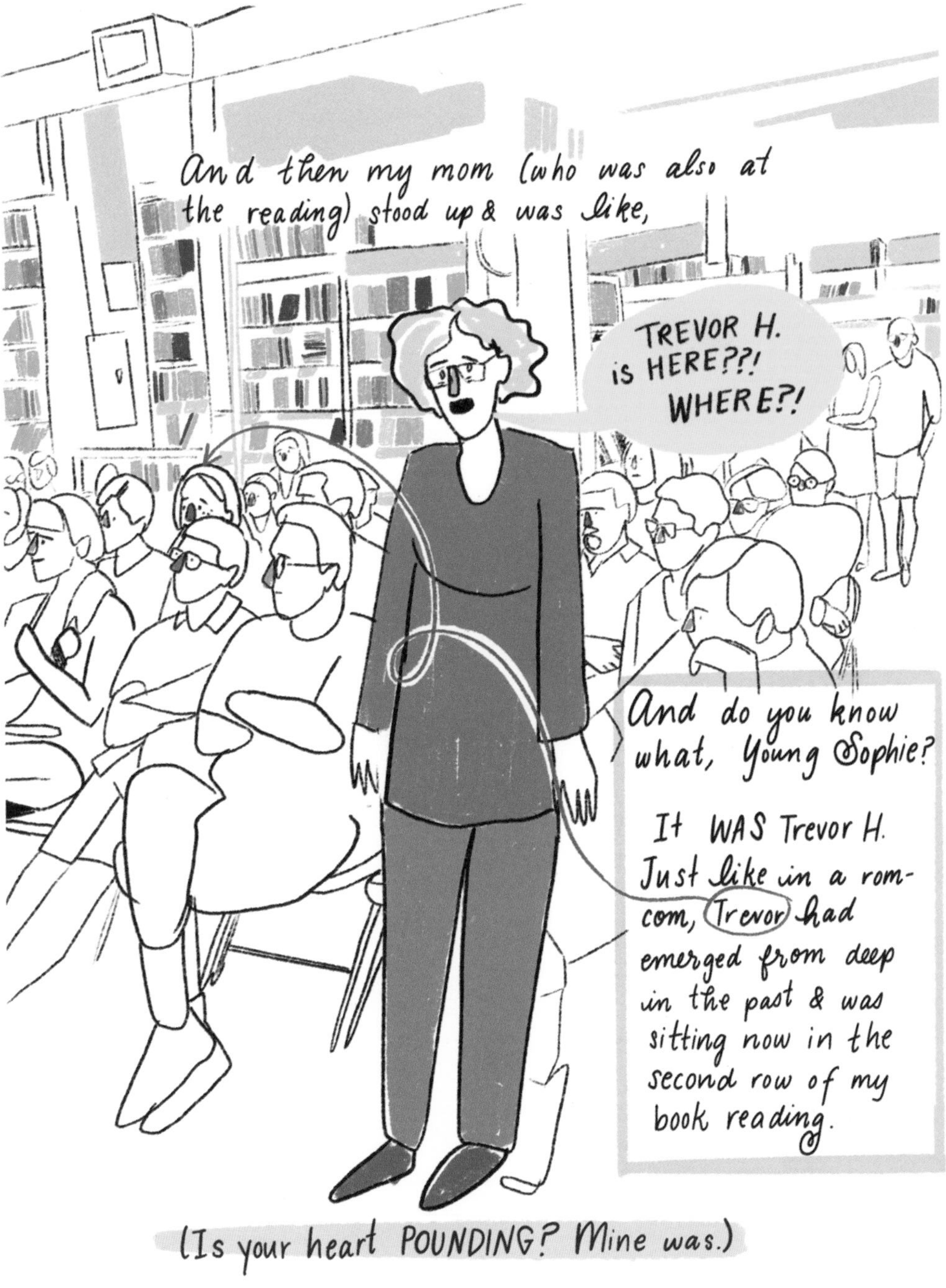
And then my mom (who was also at the reading) stood up & was like,
TREVOR H. is HERE??! WHERE?!
And do you know what, Young Sophie?
It WAS Trevor H. Just like in a rom-com, Trevor had emerged from deep in the past & was sitting now in the second row of my book reading.
(Is your heart POUNDING? Mine was.)

After the reading, Trevor invited me over to have lunch the next day.

I met Trevor's wife, who was beautiful & sharp. When I visited, she'd been making clay vases that looked like fat bodies; she did activism around body positivity.

Together, we made a salad, incorporating things they'd grown in their very own backyard.

THIS IS WHEN I ASKED TREVOR ABOUT NOT LOVING YOU.

To be fair, I didn't ask that EXACTLY.

I asked Trevor,

SO, WHAT'S GOING ON IN YOUR LIFE?

OK, no, you're right: that's not the same thing. But the answer spoke to both questions.

WELL. I'M TRANSITIONING! I'M GENDERQUEER.

They talked about how they'd never felt comfortable in their own body, being in the world as a boy.

They didn't feel comfortable when you two knew each other, just _being_ _themselves_.

They said they felt shame. They said they didn't know how to be, nor did they want to be opened up.

39

Young Sophie, here is what Trevor didn't love about you:

Nothing.

Trevor was actually not thinking about you very much at all. Trevor was thinking about Trevor, & their thoughts were hard, & confusing, & impossible for them to translate to you or to anyone else.

In fact, no one is ever thinking about you nearly as much as you think that they are. They have their own lives to worry about.

This is a wonderful relief.

So, to speak to your fears from 2 entries ago:

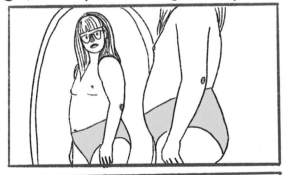

THERE WAS NOTHING WRONG WITH YOUR BOOBS.

THERE WAS NOTHING WRONG WITH YOUR WEIGHT.

THERE WAS NOTHING WRONG WITH YOUR NOSE.

There was nothing wrong with you at all.

Love, Sophie

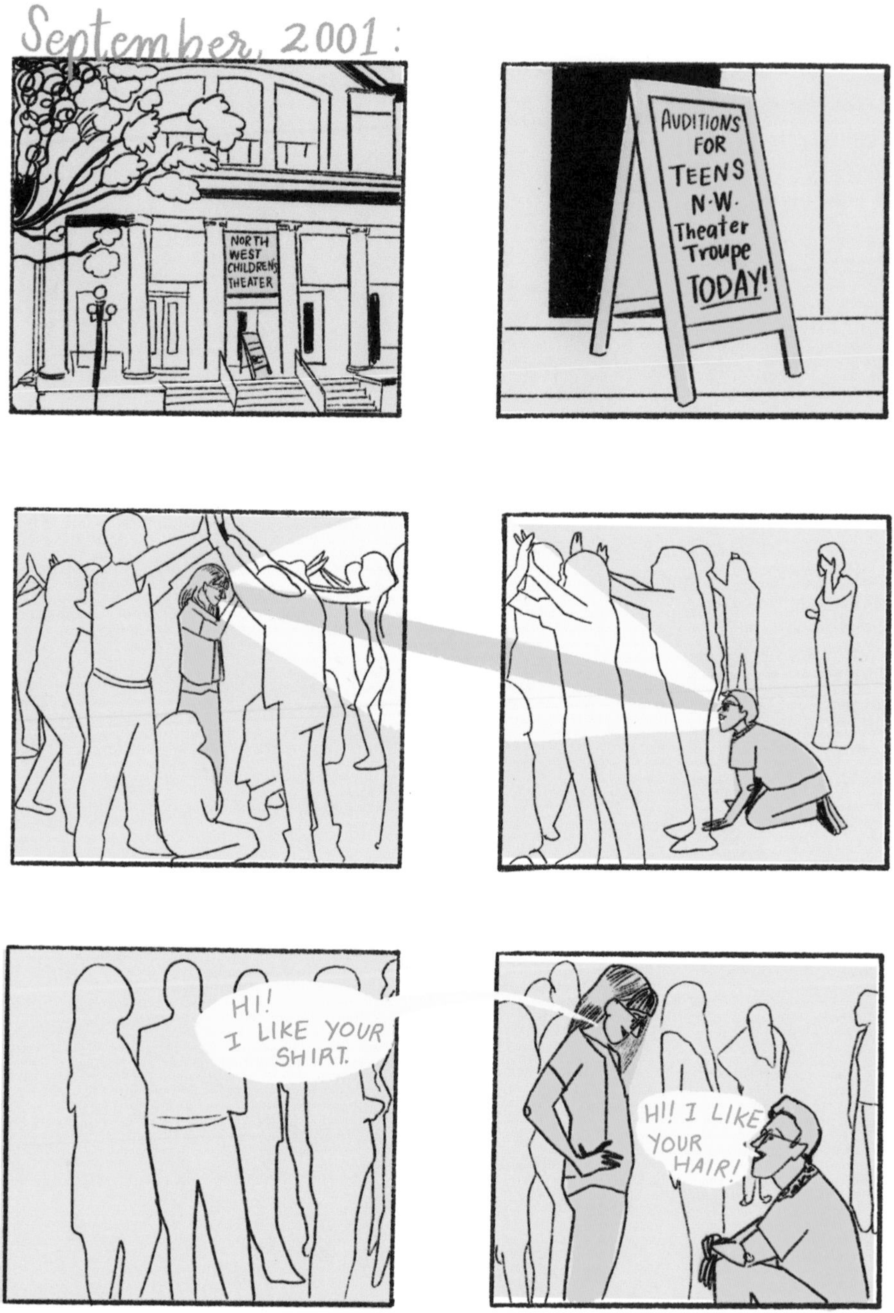
September, 2001:
NORTH WEST CHILDREN'S THEATER
AUDITIONS FOR TEENS N·W· Theater Troupe TODAY!
HI! I LIKE YOUR SHIRT.
HI!! I LIKE YOUR HAIR!

9/16/2001

Dear Diary,

A conversation I just had on AIM:

Sophie: Do you have a girlfriend?
Wonderful Eli: No. Do you have a boyfriend?
Sophie: No. I never have.
Wonderful Eli: Me either. Girlfriend.
Sophie: Do you ever feel like the last one alive?
Wonderful Eli: Yes!
Sophie: We lead pathetic lives.
Wonderful Eli: I know.
Sophie: If it makes you feel better, I'd go out with you.
Wonderful Eli: Aww! That's so sweet!
Sophie: I'm just being honest.
Wonderful Eli: How about it then?

♡

OH MY GOD
MY LIFE IS THE BEST!
IT IS THE **BEST**!
REMEMBER WHEN IT SUCKED?

WELL, IT DOESN'T
ANYMORE! I'M SO
HAPPY!!!!!!!!!

LOVE,   ♡
Sophie

Dear Sophie,
And then you fell in love. It seemed like you were CONSUMED by this love.

For the period you were in love with Eli, you were the happiest & saddest that it is possible for your human body to be.

Yesterday, I drew THESE PICTURES & put them online:

You guys ever think, "WOW

NO ONE EVER REALLY APPRECIATED MY WHIMSICAL LOVE OF DANDELIONS THE WAY I'D BANKED ON?"

And Eli left a comment on the picture:

eli_says: We may have been in high school, but I remember appreciating it a lot.

ELI'S REAL SCREEN NAME IS A REFERENCE TO A CAMPY HORROR MOVIE. I KNOW YOU'LL HATE THIS, & I AM SORRY.

I read this comment & felt a tether in my chest,

& wouldn't you know it, tears welled up in my (adult!) eyes.

There it was: the ghost of how it felt to be so head-over-heels in love with a person the way you are with Eli now.

Young Sophie, your impulse that maybe a feeling so large does not ever go away

is right.

I WONDER WHEN THOSE FEELINGS GO FROM BEING living feelings TO BEING ghosts.

My sadness reading the comment came from knowing you only get

your first love

one time,

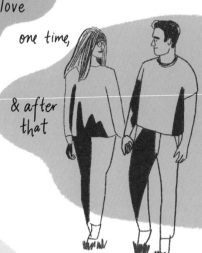

& after that

all the rest of the loves

are a little...

less.

But you, Young Sophie, seemed to know this as it was happening. Every moment that that love was exploding through its spring, you appreciated it. You wished you could stop time.

The ghosts you've left me with are BRIGHT & PALPABLE & make me cry when I read comments from my ex-boyfriend on the internet. (It can be nice to cry.)

I COULDN'T BE MORE GRATEFUL.

Thank you for being wise enough to savor.

My life right now is full of moments — WONDERFUL ONES — that I neglect to hold as they come.

WHEN IT'S SUMMER & I'M HAVING WATERMELON IN THE BACKYARD OF THE HOUSE I BOUGHT & REBUILT WITH MY HUSBAND.

WHEN THE CATS FALL ASLEEP ON MY BELLY IN THE AFTERNOON.

WHEN I SEE AN OWL.

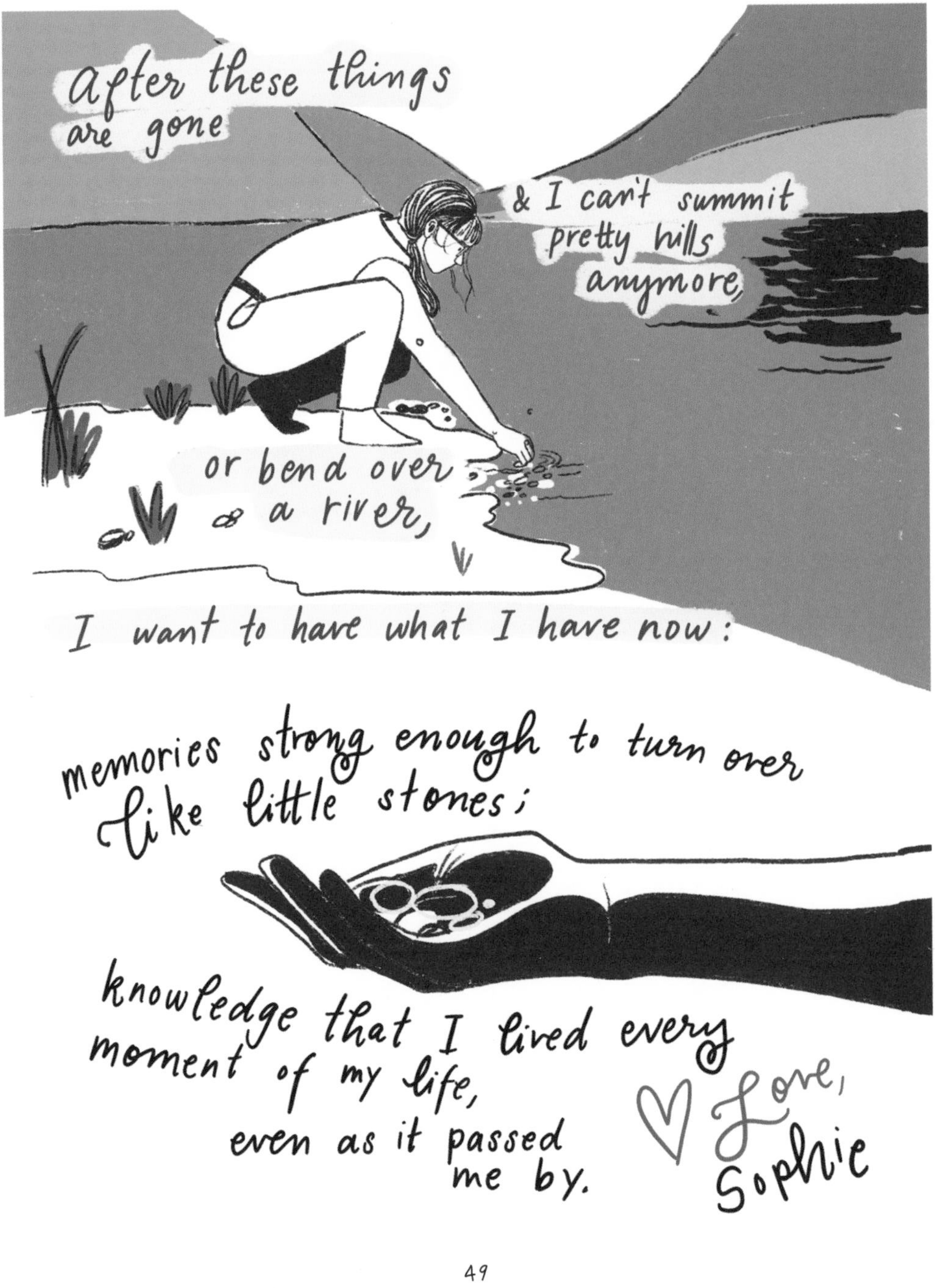
after these things are gone
& I can't summit pretty hills anymore,
or bend over a river,
I want to have what I have now:
memories strong enough to turn over like little stones;
knowledge that I lived every moment of my life, even as it passed me by.
Love, Sophie

1/28/2002

Dear Diary,

Any pride I ever had was shattered yesterday when, embarrassing moment of embarrassing moments, I touched Eli's penis. I don't want to build up to it when the truth of the matter is the penis has been touched. I thought it was a spool of thread, okay?! He simply said, "Hey, you shouldn't be poking that," and I dissolved into nervous, obnoxious, compulsive laughter, only heightening my extreme embarrassment. COME ON! Is he SUPPOSED to get a hard-on when all we do is kiss? Ew! Maybe I should find this sexy or attractive, but... EWWWW! The only good thing I can gather from this is, well, I think he didn't exactly hate that I touched his penis, if you know what I mean.

And then I went to Deb's house, and Deb has a girl-friend now. And they are cute together. One thing that would be good about being a lesbian would be that you wouldn't have to touch anyone's penis.

Love,
Sophie

Dear Sophie,

I'll catch some *flak* for saying this but:

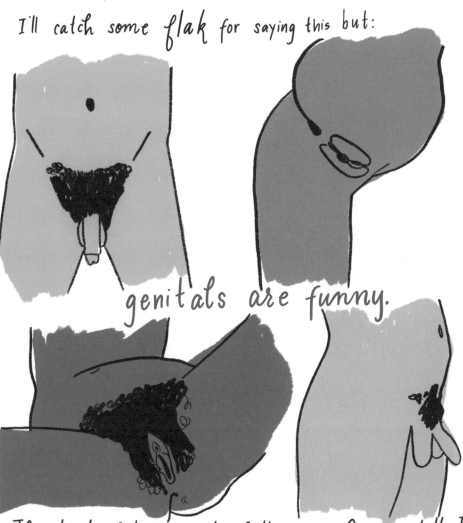

genitals are funny.

They kind of have minds of their own. As an adult, I still think genitals are more funny than they are anything else, and this has greatly embarrassed a lot of people I've dated.

Love, Sophie

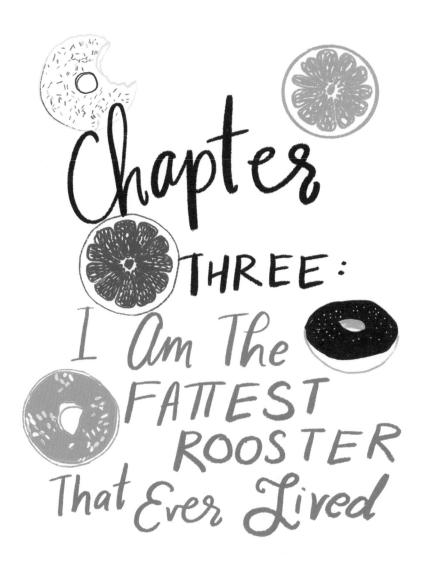

Chapter

THREE:

I Am The
FATTEST
ROOSTER
That Ever Lived

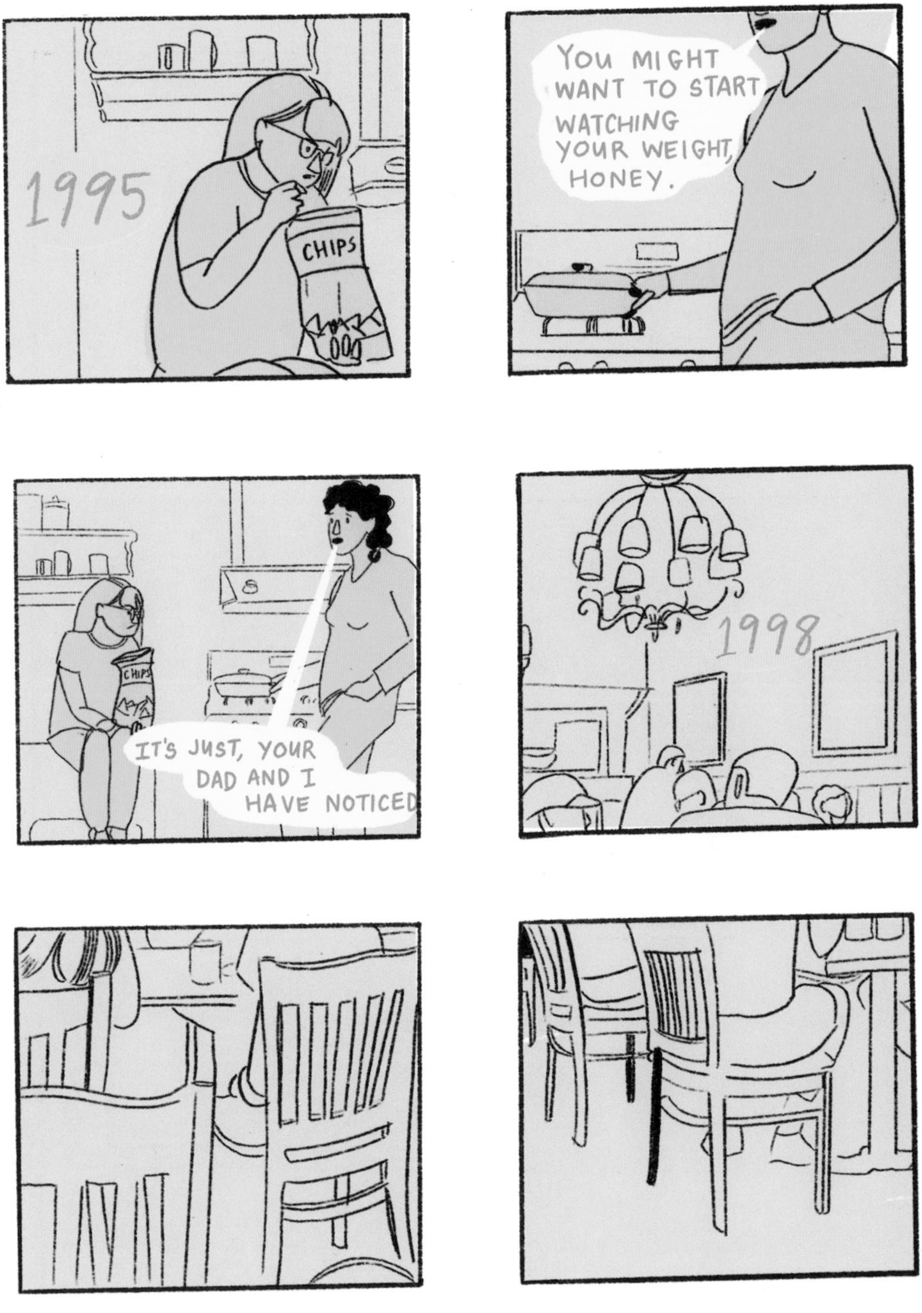
1995
CHIPS
YOU MIGHT WANT TO START WATCHING YOUR WEIGHT, HONEY.
CHIPS
IT'S JUST, YOUR DAD AND I HAVE NOTICED
1998

SOPHIE, I WANT TO SHOW YOU SOMETHING. COME WITH ME.

ISN'T THAT SAD?

LOOK HOW BIG SHE GOT!

AND THAT COULD HAPPEN TO YOU IF YOU'RE NOT CAREFUL.

1999

I MADE YOU AN APPOINTMENT WITH A NUTRITIONIST.

WE'RE GOING TO GET THIS UNDER CONTROL.

2000

HOW ABOUT SOME SALAD, SOPH?

SALAD AND RUNNING. THAT'S THE TICKET!

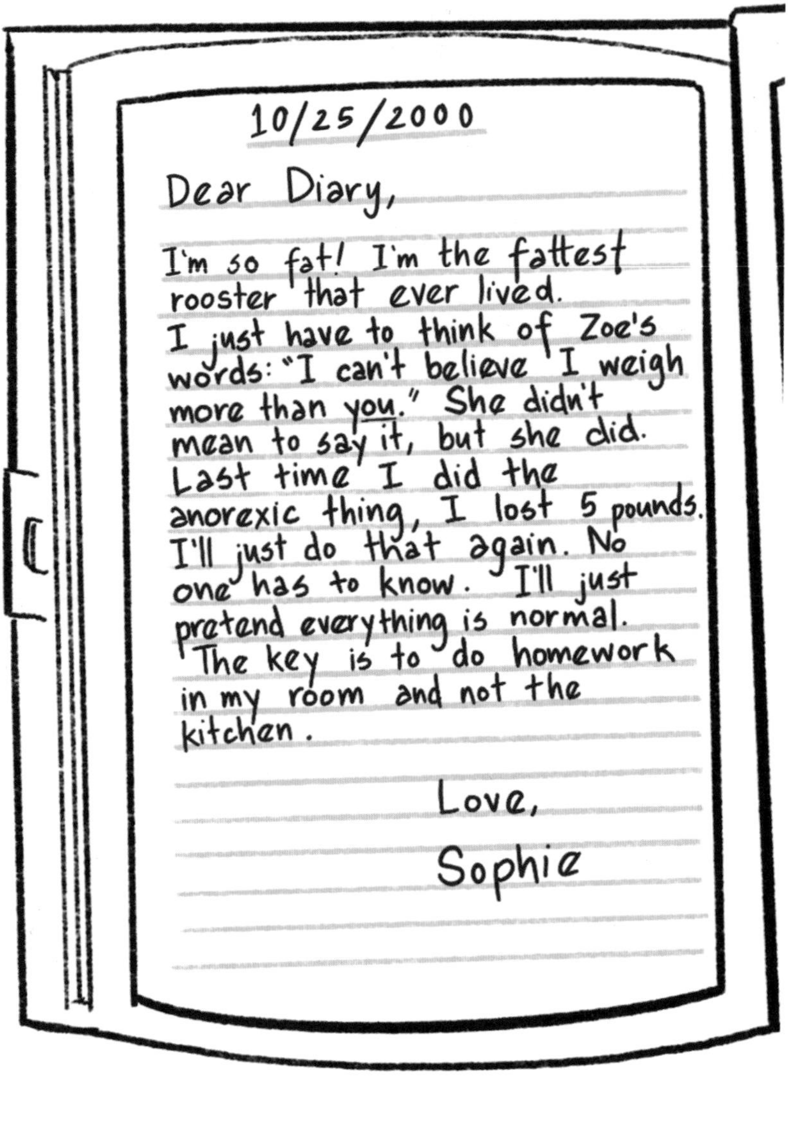
10/25/2000
Dear Diary,
I'm so fat! I'm the fattest rooster that ever lived.
I just have to think of Zoe's words: "I can't believe I weigh more than you." She didn't mean to say it, but she did.
Last time I did the anorexic thing, I lost 5 pounds.
I'll just do that again. No one has to know. I'll just pretend everything is normal.
The key is to do homework in my room and not the kitchen.
Love,
Sophie

Dear Sophie,

I wish I could say,

GREAT NEWS! I am now exactly the size I want to be.

I NEVER think about my weight anymore.

I've re-allocated that energy toward SOCIAL JUSTICE!

But the truth is I still think about my body and how much it weighs literally every day.

I HATE THAT THIS IS TRUE.

IT IS POISONOUS & WASTEFUL.

It MAKES ME FEEL LIKE I'M BROKEN.

Over the years, I've been told that there are a lot of "keys" to losing weight.

THE KEY IS TO

CUT OUT SUGAR.

THE KEY IS TO GO RUNNING EVERY MORNING (which I hate) SO THAT I'LL REMEMBER ALL DAY HOW HARD I WORKED & HOW NOT-WORTH-IT IT IS TO EAT A DOUGHNUT.

THE KEY IS TO BECOME A VEGAN.
TELL EVERYONE

It's political!

EAT LOTS OF

PLAIN LETTUCE!

DRINK DIET SODA!

OR BETTER YET, SPARKLING WATER!

OR BETTER YET, REGULAR WATER!

PUT LEMON IN YOUR FOOD SO YOU WON'T WANT TO GOBBLE IT DOWN SO QUICKLY.

LEAVE PARTIES BEFORE THEY BRING OUT THE CAKE.

DON'T KEEP ANYTHING "SNACKY" IN THE HOUSE.

THE KEY IS TO REWARD YOURSELF WHEN YOU MEET A goal weight. After you meet a goal weight, you should set a new one.

AS AN INTERIM REWARD, BUY YOURSELF A NEW WATER BOTTLE OR SIGN UP FOR AN EXPENSIVE YOGA CLASS.

YOU CANNOT REWARD YOURSELF WITH PIZZA, WHICH IS THE ONLY THING YOU REALLY WANT.

THE KEY IS TO WEAR A RUBBER BAND AROUND YOUR WRIST

AND SNAP IT REALLY HARD EVERY TIME YOU ARE ABOUT TO GO FOR AN M&M FROM A DISH, OR A COOKIE AT A MEETING.

Currently, I am counting calories.

It seems to be the simplest & most effective way to ensure weight loss.

It's hard for me to not eat at night, because I'm an emotional eater & the nighttime is an emotional time— so my solution is to try not to eat for as much of the morning as possible.

Today I made it to about noon.

Then I had

MICRO GREENS
(12 calories)

1 EGG (FROM MY
own CHICKENS, SO
IT'S NOT AN UNETHICAL
EGG, DON'T WORRY;
80 calories)

½ SMALL
AVOCADO
(120 calories)

1 PIECE SEEDED
RYE BREAD
(130 calories)

I also had some

CARROT JUICE
(70 calories)

for a "treat."

I can do calorie-adding math in my head incredibly quickly now. So at least I'm improving at math, even if I will never meet my goal weight.

"Goal weight" is a number that does not exist.

The other thing that counting calories is really good for is ruining 🌀 how much you enjoy the things you eat.

IT'S GOOD FOR MAKING DINNER PARTIES FEEL TERRIFYING, because you don't know if the host used butter or oil, Meaning that you can't get an accurate number.

It is an excellent way to take one of the greatest pleasures in life —eating delicious food— & siphon 80 percent of the joy out of it.

IT BECOMES AN OBSESSION THAT FEELS IMPOSSIBLE TO STOP.

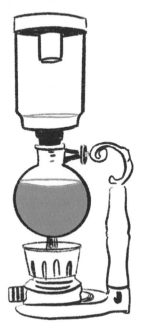

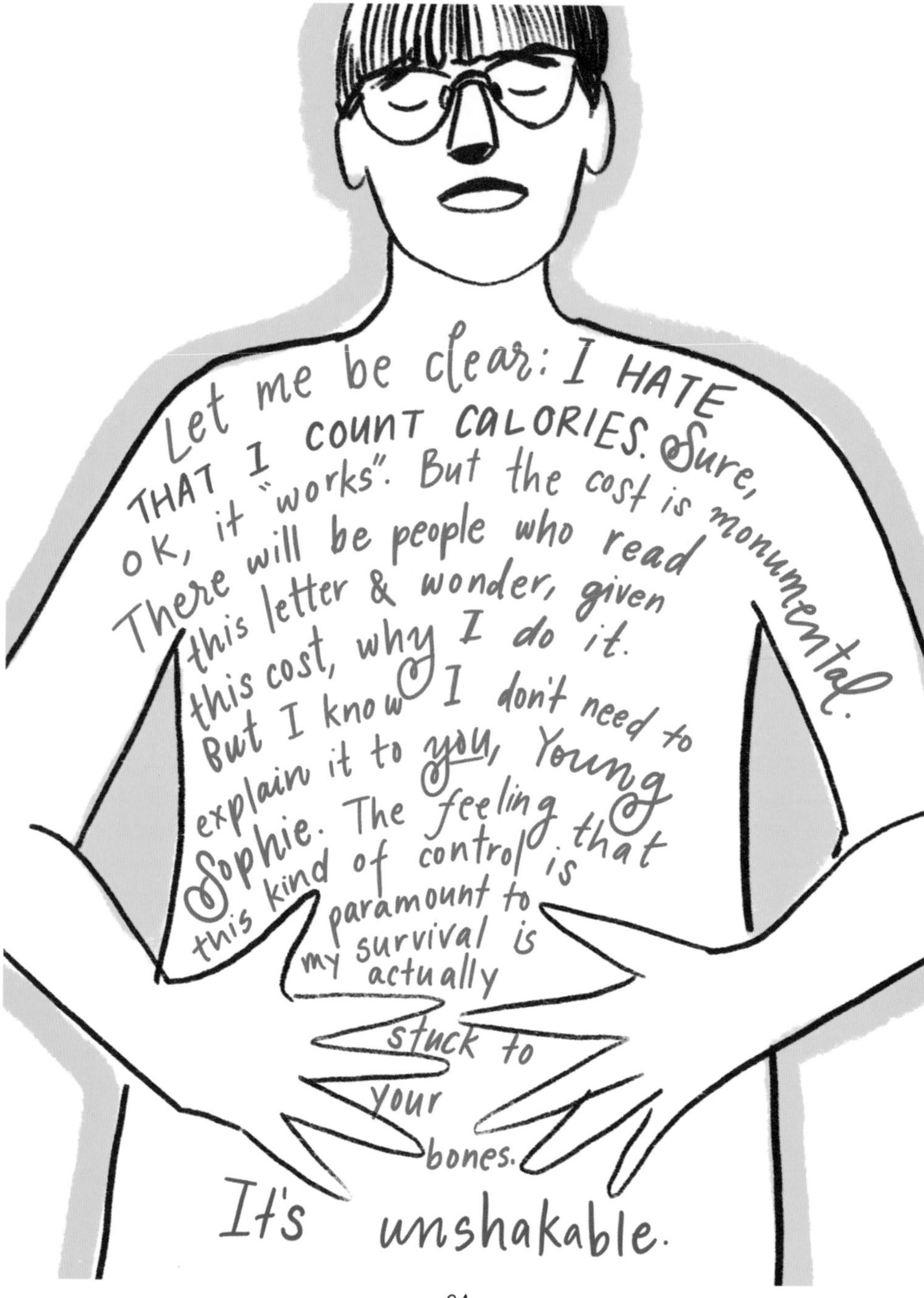
Let me be clear: I HATE THAT I COUNT CALORIES. Sure, OK, it "works". But the cost is monumental.
There will be people who read this letter & wonder, given this cost, why I do it.
But I know I don't need to explain it to you, Young Sophie. The feeling that this kind of control is paramount to my survival is actually stuck to your bones.
It's unshakable.

What I'm describing, & what you were describing, is textbook disordered eating. I've sought therapy for it. I've talked to SUPPORT GROUPS. The social consensus seems to be,

IT DOESN'T REALLY COUNT IF YOU'RE GENERALLY HEALTHY & YOUR HABIT ISN'T LIFE-THREATENING.

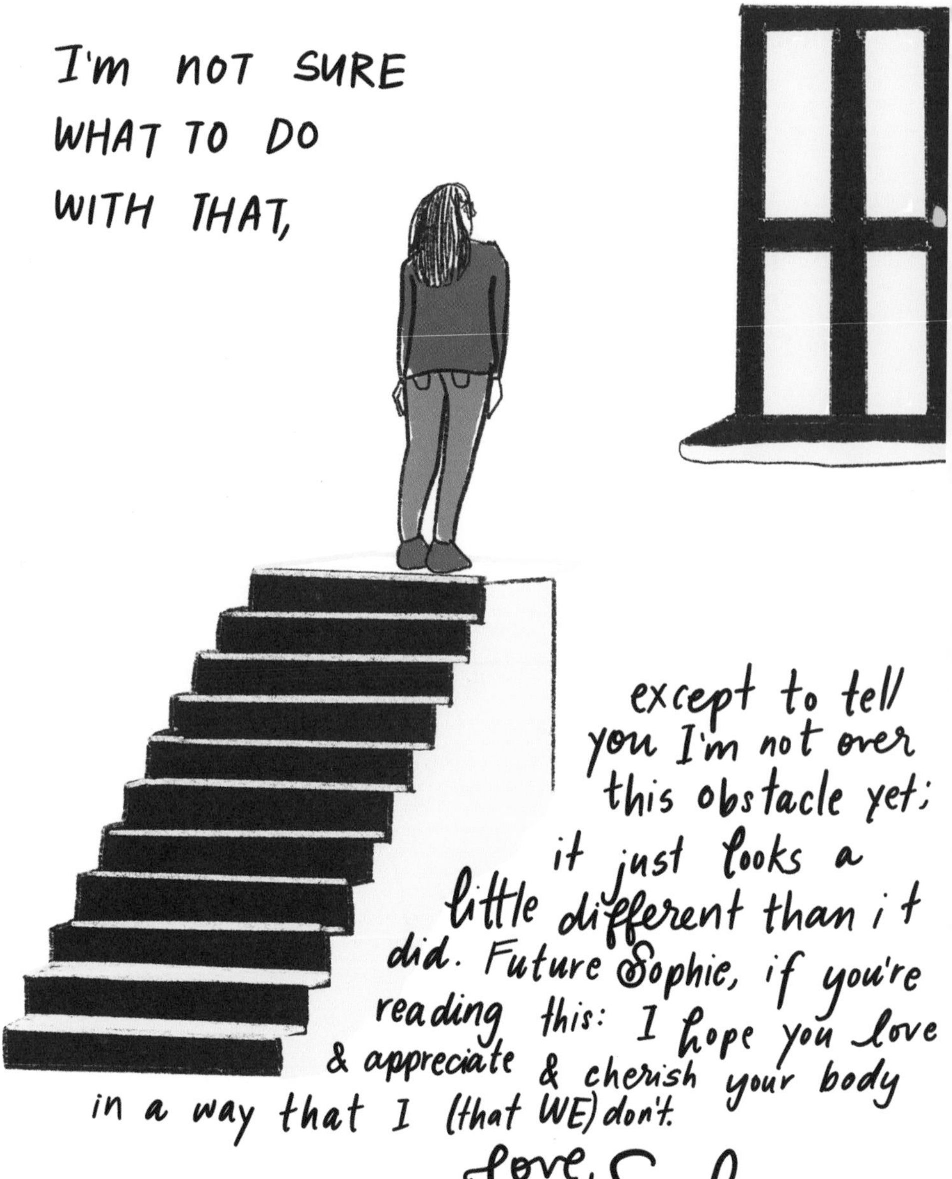
I'M NOT SURE WHAT TO DO WITH THAT,
except to tell you I'm not over this obstacle yet; it just looks a little different than it did. Future Sophie, if you're reading this: I hope you love & appreciate & cherish your body in a way that I (that WE) don't.
Love, Sophie

08/20/2001

Dear Diary,

Metabolism is so stupid. I hate it. I hate mine, specifically. But that's the way life goes. I only ran a mile and a half tonight 'cause it got dark early. FUCKING METABOLISM! It keeps me from reaching my goal.

I realized today that I am hideously ugly. Perhaps this is why I could never get Trevor. I have this bulky masculine nose and this repulsive double chin and glasses shielding my lovely eyes. Plus, I'm abnormally fat. I cheated and ate a doughnut today. If I want to be a vegan I have to BE A VEGAN, dammit.

Why does my family even BUY doughnuts? It ruins my life.

Love,

Sophie

Dear Sophie,

If I could choose between

BEING THIN & TONED FOR THE REST OF MY LIFE

&

HONESTLY NOT CARING ABOUT WHAT SIZE MY BODY WAS,

I would choose the latter.

The amount of time I've wasted — WE'VE wasted, because at fourteen you've already wasted So. Much. Time. — worrying about the shape & size of my body is as astounding as it is shameful.

And it's not the fault of your metabolism, nor is it the fault of doughnuts in general.

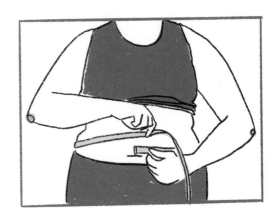

It's that for the first 14 years of your life,

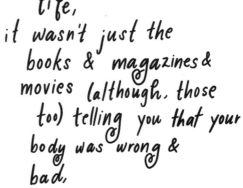

it wasn't just the books & magazines & movies (although, those too) telling you that your body was wrong & bad,

BUT IT WAS ALSO THE PEOPLE WHO LOVED YOU.

They were trying to look out for you.

They believed that it was hard out there for a fat girl.

And more infuriating than anything else is

THEY WERE RIGHT.

Because as soon as you lose the weight—

WHICH YOU WILL; SHORTLY AFTER YOU WRITE THIS ENTRY

YOU'RE GOING TO STOP EATING PRETTY MUCH
ALTOGETHER FOR TWO YEARS—

people are nicer to you, boys pay attention to you, you start to get elected to leadership positions at school, your family can't stop telling you how proud they are of you.

And that feels good.

For your part, you put on that Fiona Apple album & fast-forward to the "Paper Bag" track over & over again, repeating the lyrics when you feel weak:

You believe —
& in a deep & chemical way, I probably still believe — that you

deserve
to
hurt.

There are womxn in my life now who
seem like they've freed themselves
from the perpetual prison of
fundamentally believing their
bodies are in the public domain.
Womxn are writing about this now;
they're taking their agency back.

SO MANY OTHERS.

All this amazing writing makes me feel
more hopeful, & less alone.

Less alone,
but it hasn't
taken away
the suffering.

It's ongoing.

What I
wouldn't give
to go a whole day
without thinking about what I ate &
how that would affect how I am going to look.

Love,
Sophie

11/4/2001

Dear Diary,

Am I ever going to sprout a pair of breasts? All the other girls have them. No. ALL the other girls. I do not. You'd think all the fat in my body decided to just skip its way through my body right to my gigantic stomach, completely forgetting the space in my bustle area. I wish I had some boobs. My sister Alexis has a larger chest than I do. By a LOT. You know, one day, the whole WonderBra thing is going to suddenly stop working. Some guy is going to want to see my rack or lack thereof and will realize I have a manly bosom. No guy will ever date me again. It's only a matter of time, you know. Eli would not love me if he knew I can't even boast an A-cup. I keep expecting to wake up in the morning and have fat in the womanly places. IF ONLY I HAD A SET OF BREASTS.

Love,

Sophie

Dear Sophie,

I have bad news & I have good news.

The bad news is that you don't ever really "sprout a pair of breasts." You are a person who has small breasts. You will never— at least not as far as I know— need a bra that has a cup. You actually don't really <u>need</u> a bra at all.

THESE ARE MY BREASTS! I love them.

And that's the good news! Small breasts <u>RULE</u>. I wish I could have told you that a <u>LOT</u> sooner.

(Actually, <u>all</u> breasts rule! But let me tell you what's so great about small ones.)

First of all, boys don't really seem to care that much about the size of your boobs; they're just pleased they get to be naked with you.

Second, I can't emphasize enough how nice it is to be able to go on long runs without anything BOUNCING.

Third, give it about a decade & BRALETTES will come into style. You are going to be able to pull those off GREAT.

Fourth, Eli would have loved you even if you didn't have a torso. He was a catch in that way.

Prepare to enjoy the following things more than any other girl you know:

HALTER TOPS.

TINY BATH-ING SUITS.

JUMPING UP& DOWN AT CONCERTS.

ANSWERING BOYS WHO ARE LIKE, Can I put my penis between your tits?

BECAUSE THE ANSWER WILL BE, Physically? No. AND YOU'LL LIKE THAT.

Love, Sophie

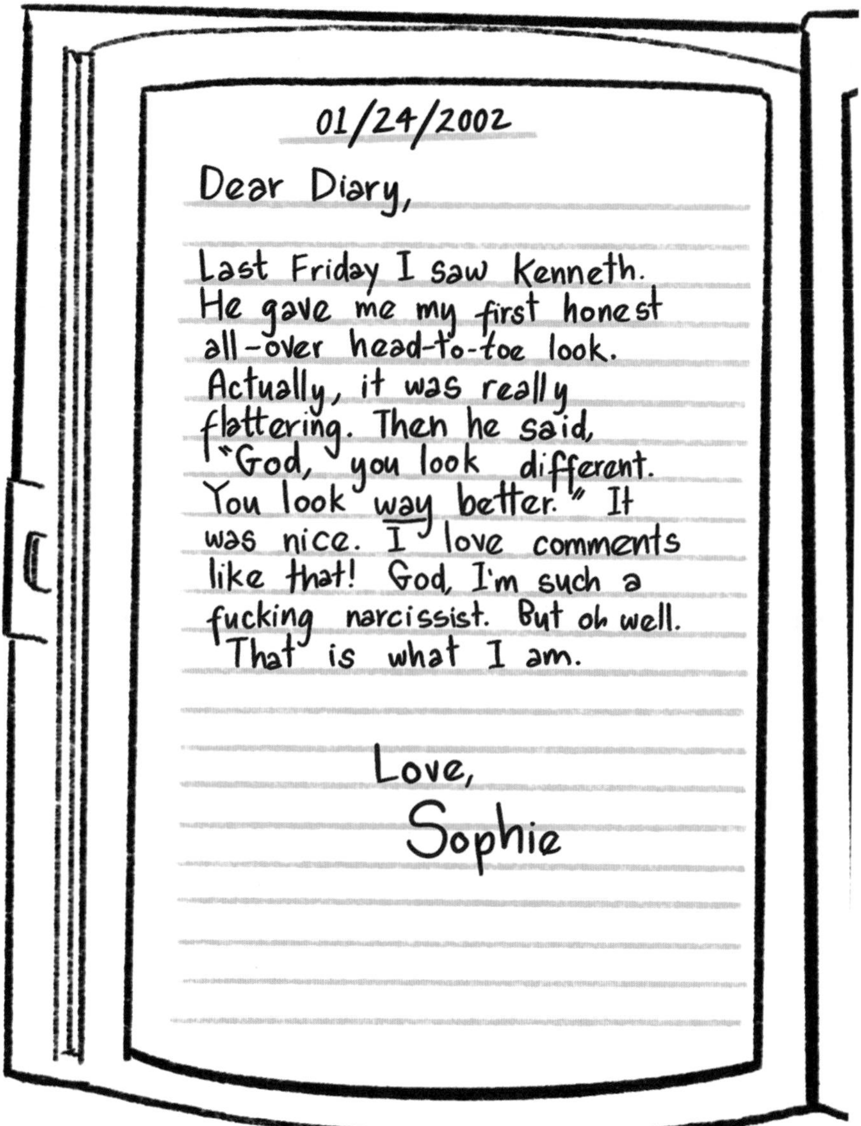
01/24/2002
Dear Diary,
Last Friday I saw Kenneth. He gave me my first honest all-over head-to-toe look. Actually, it was really flattering. Then he said, "God, you look different. You look way better." It was nice. I love comments like that! God, I'm such a fucking narcissist. But oh well. That is what I am.
Love,
Sophie

Dear Sophie,
Ugh. Fucking Kenneth.

See, this is what I mean when I refer to being in a "PERPETUAL PRISON OF FUNDAMENTALLY BELIEVING YOUR BODY IS IN THE PUBLIC DOMAIN."

It's so infuriating that Kenneth felt like he was entitled to an opinion about your body.

And we—the collective we—imbue comments like these with so much value that we actually never forget about them.

In fact, no one should get to say anything about your body, ever.
OK, three exceptions:

1) Your doctor can say things about your body, because that is her job.

2) Your lover can say things about your body, but they should be things like,

Wow, YOUR BODY IS GETTING ME SO HOT & TURNED ON RIGHT NOW.

WHOa, YOUR BODY PARTS FEEL GREAT TO TOUCH!

3) If you've been recently & publicly sick, a person might ask,

HOW IS YOUR BODY FEELING?

There is a fourth exception, which is unlikely, but maybe bears listing: if it seems like you're turning into a werewolf — & THIS HAS TO BE BLATANTLY OBVIOUS; LIKE, YOU HAVE TO HAVE A TAIL, PRETTY MUCH — your friends might be like,

Hey, is your body maybe turning into a werewolf?

But that's IT.
There are No. Other. Exceptions.

My friend Rachel recently got diagnosed with Crohn's disease, & she went to the dentist after battling this grim, unpleasant, heartbreaking disease for over a year. Her dentist said,

WHOA! YOU'VE LOST WEIGHT.

YEAH, I WAS DIAGNOSED WITH CROHN'S.

I GUESS THERE'S SOME SILVER LINING!

This HAPPENED.

In the year 2020.

And this is exactly it: women are openly encouraged to ACTUALLY BECOME PHYSICALLY SICK if it means that they might lose weight.

I know this is a punch line in a lot of "FUNNY-'CAUSE-IT'S-TRUE" women's humor, but think about it for a second.

Rachel has chronic diarrhea, stomachaches, & is so fatigued she can't do half the things she used to do. BUT AT LEAST SHE'S FUCKING SKINNY.

That's actually not *funny* at all.

The tricky thing is that I can know all of this in my brain without ~~feeling~~ like it's true. I can say,

SOPHIE, YOU'RE STRONG. YOUR BODY CAN TAKE YOU FROM PLACE TO PLACE, & YOU CAN LIFT HEAVY BOXES. YOU ALMOST NEVER GET SICK. YOUR BODY IS A-1 TOP NOTCH, BECAUSE EVEN THOUGH YOU BERATE IT & PUT IT DOWN & STARVE IT, IT CONTINUES TO SHOW UP FOR YOU. BE GRATEFUL.

And even so, I know you'll hear me without really hearing. I know this because I'm the same way.

So all I can say is:

DO BETTER FOR THE GIRLS WHO COME AFTER YOU.

Teach them that they're good enough just the
way they are. Let them eat things that
bring them joy. Wait as long as you possibly
can before you use the word "calorie" around them.

And hope they'll listen.

Love,
Sophie

Chapter FOUR:

Weird Al Is a Very Neat Guy

08 / 4 / 2000

Dear Diary,

I went to a Weird Al concert tonight. It was SO good. Weird Al is a very neat guy. I would happily marry him right now. I was screaming so loud I completely lost my voice, but oh well. The concert was sort of a freak show with hilarious video clips in between (when Weird Al was changing costumes). There were several RABID Weird Al fans in the audience. I am maniacally in love with Weird Al, but some people were just in COMPLETE adoration of him. He rocks.

I am convinced that Rider Strong, Johnny Rzeznik, and Weird Al watch me through my window and argue about who will get to ask me to marry them.

Don't shatter this.

Love,

Sophie

8/8/2000

Dear Diary,

Today was oh-so-sweet! Although camp was long and stressful, I stayed up to eleven so I could watch The List on VH1. WEIRD AL was the host. I just KNOW Alexis is angry at me for falling in love with him, but I just can't help it! He's amazing! He was wearing really hot pants, too. Leopard spotted, shiny black ones. Sigh.

Too bad he's in love with his best friend. I think I read that somewhere.

Hey...Joe could learn from him!

Love,
Sophie

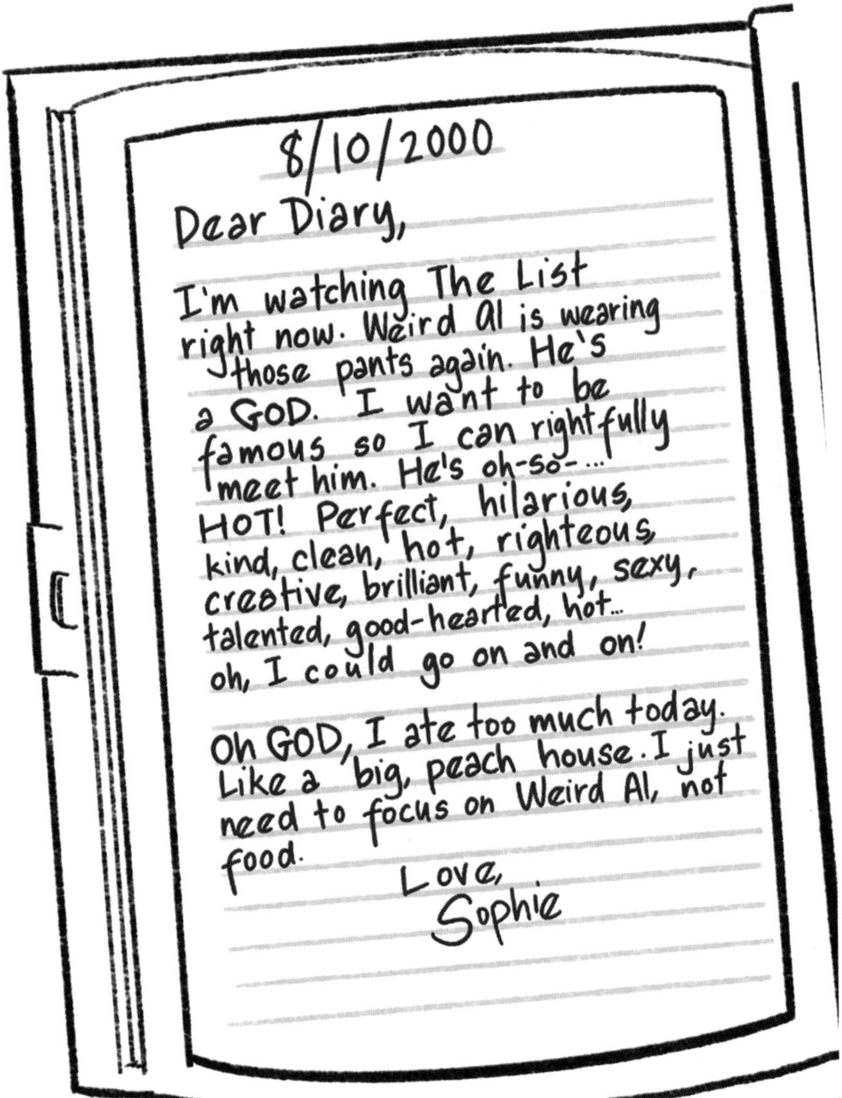
8/10/2000
Dear Diary,
I'm watching The List
right now. Weird Al is wearing
those pants again. He's
a GOD. I want to be
famous so I can rightfully
meet him. He's oh-so-...
HOT! Perfect, hilarious,
kind, clean, hot, righteous,
creative, brilliant, funny, sexy,
talented, good-hearted, hot...
oh, I could go on and on!
Oh GOD, I ate too much today.
Like a big, peach house. I just
need to focus on Weird Al, not
food.
Love,
Sophie

Dear Sophie,

If you can believe it, it is still cool to like Weird Al. It's arguably a lot cooler. Someone recently wrote a whole article about it for <u>The New York Times Magazine</u> that made me incredibly jealous, because I felt I could have written it even better, but oh well, it's <u>The New York Times Magazine</u>'s loss, I think.

While I really have enjoyed writing you letters, Young Sophie, I would like to depart for a moment here & write instead to someone else.

Someone we both know & love.

Dear Weird Al,
    Here is what you gave me when I was fourteen:
you gave me a new way to exist in the world.

Before I got to know
you, I thought a person
was either   **a winner**

OR

a loser.

You either
succeeded
at the
things that
had been
culturally
agreed upon
as Important
or you failed.

For a girl, these things
were : •OWNING A NORTH FACE JACKET,
    •KNOWING INFORMATION ABOUT *NSYNC
    •GETTING YOUR CRUSH TO LIKE YOU
    •DOING A REALLY GOOD HIGH PONYTAIL
    •BEING ABLE TO EFFORTLESSLY APPLY & WEAR PINK LIPGLOSS & GLITTER
&•HAVING A COOL BOYFRIEND WHO ALSO WORE A NORTH FACE JACKET

Of these milestones, I had,
by the age of fourteen, achieved zero.
I sulked a lot about being a loser.

Every day I'd wake up & try to accomplish the Important things & I'd fail all over again.

Then I saw your episode of

VH1 BEHIND THE MUSIC

Two things came into focus:

One was that
you didn't seem
to be interested in
achieving the Important
things;

& the other was that
you had a whole lot
of friends.

At the end of the day, you were aggressively nice
while simultaneously never taking yourself or anyone around you
too seriously. It started to occur to me that I too might be able
to _fit in_ by choosing _not to fit in._

This is not a particularly unique revelation, & I could have learned it by getting into

RAGE AGAINST THE MACHINE or even

THE EARLY STIRRINGS OF DASHBOARD CONFESSIONAL

But instead I learned it from you.

And because I learned it from you, Weird Al, I put a lot of effort into being nice & being funny.

Because I kept these tenets in mind, my life turned all the way around.

For me,

there is a

Before AI

&

an After AI

& you are the
pivotal hinge where
my life completely
changed.

I really feel like I
bet on the right horse,
Weird AI.

I still think you're sexy & hot, & I love that you & I
are both vegans.

I appreciate you now & always.

Love, Sophie

PS· I want to thank you for teaching me so much about <u>Star Wars</u>. I know a lot of <u>Star Wars</u> trivia without having to have to actually <u>seen</u> any <u>Star Wars</u> movies. This has worked out for me on many dates with a certain kind of man.

Chapter FIVE:
I've Never Felt Like That About a Girl Before

10/1/2000

Dear Diary,

I have never been more happy in my entire life. Not once. Everything is wonderful. I am so contented about myself, my position, my dreams, my entire... life! I know that sounds corny and stupid, but I'm just so glad about everything. My soul is free.

I had an amazing weekend at the beach with Joe. He told me he was gay, and I think it's wonderful. Everything seems clearer; it all makes sense. It's amazing how much I complained that he didn't tell me anything. Oh, oh, oh, oh how STUPID! I had no IDEA how serious some people's issues are. I really am quite egotistical. I do wish he had told me sooner, though. I could have been so supportive. I realize, however, that I have the chance to be supportive NOW.

And do you know why he said he told Debbie first? Because he cares more about my friendship than he does about his friendship with Debbie. I admire him for coming out, and for being happy about his life. I think he is a brave hero.

And he has really great taste in guys! He is even more open about it than any of my girlfriends. After he told me, everything in my life is different. He is so much more honest, so much more loose. He can cuddle with me!

Last night, we snuck out of the house around midnight and we clutched arms and walked and talked in the dark. We got scared,

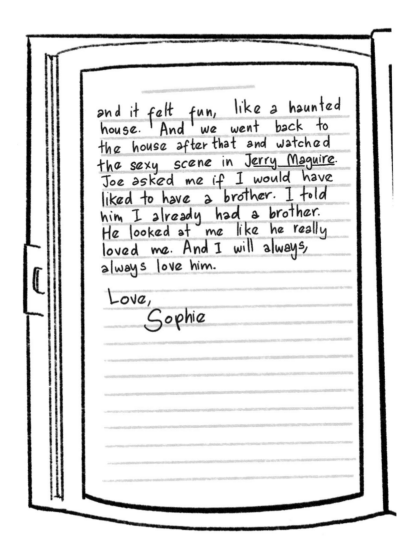

and it felt fun, like a haunted house. And we went back to the house after that and watched the sexy scene in Jerry Maguire. Joe asked me if I would have liked to have a brother. I told him I already had a brother. He looked at me like he really loved me. And I will always, always love him.

Love,
    Sophie

Dear Sophie,

This was a big deal.

It's hard sometimes to remember that it hasn't been such a long time since coming out was a really big deal.

You were right to recognize how lucky you were to know Joe — because not only could he talk with you about cute boys and how to do good blow jobs (NECESSARY FODDER FOR A YOUNG PERSON),

but he helped you pay attention.

When, in just a few years, Portland becomes one of the first cities in the country to provide marriage licenses to gay couples, you'll skip school to go to the courthouse to be a witness.

And when a judge orders that practice to stop just two months later, you'll be all the more infuriated about it.

JUDGE OVERTURNS RULING

NO MORE GAY MARRIAGE!

And that's because of Joe.

He was your best friend (since you were five!);

he lived down the street;

he was probably your first great love.

Joe was kind of your everything,

so what mattered to Joe mattered to Sophie.

At the high school where I teach,

more than
half of the students in my class last year
identified as queer.

I was thinking about how, when I was
their age, when I was your age, I was
just learning
what the
word

"queer"

meant. It was too scary to think about

THE WAYS IN WHICH
A WORD LIKE
THAT MIGHT RELATE
TO A PERSON LIKE ME.

Friendship's favorite environment is honesty.

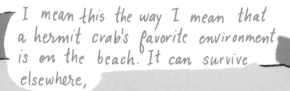

I mean this the way I mean that a hermit crab's favorite environment is on the beach. It can survive elsewhere,

BUT NOT PARTICULARLY HAPPILY.

Joe told you the truth about something scary, & it made your friendship feel whole.

Adult Joe is a filmmaker.

(This should surprise you not at all.

Remember when you starred in his self-written, self-directed, self-produced film Death Makes a Call when you were both twelve? His interest just kept on going.)

He lives in New York,

& whenever I visit the city I stay at his apartment.

Gotta hand it to him: he does have really great taste in guys. Love, Sophie.

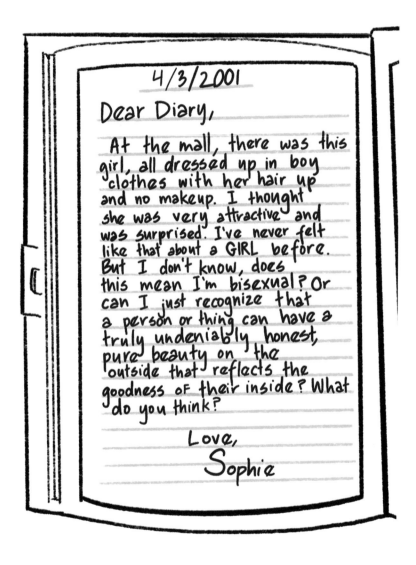

4/3/2001

Dear Diary,

At the mall, there was this girl, all dressed up in boy clothes with her hair up and no makeup. I thought she was very attractive and was surprised. I've never felt like that about a GIRL before. But I don't know, does this mean I'm bisexual? Or can I just recognize that a person or thing can have a truly undeniably honest, pure beauty on the outside that reflects the goodness of their inside? What do you think?

Love,

Sophie

Dear Sophie,

What you don't know is that in twenty years, we, culturally, will be in a much different place when it comes to gay identity & LGBT rights.

ACTUALLY, I DON'T MEAN TO BE ANNOYING ABOUT IT, BUT I USE THE ACRONYM

LGBTQIA+

now. IT'S A FEW EXTRA LETTERS, BUT IT'S REALLY NOT <u>THAT</u> MANY.

QUEER & QUESTIONING.

INTERSEX

ASEXUAL

PLUS!

which, simplified, refers to people who don't fit the typical definitions of male or female bodies.

which, simplified, refers to a person who has low or absent sexual attraction to other people.

a lot of other wonderful stratifications,

LIKE: DEMISEXUAL, GRAY SEXUAL, GENDER nonconforming, non-BINARY, PANSEXUAL, AND MORE!

I bet you're thinking,

WOW!
HOW COOL THAT IN
THE FUTURE THERE
ARE SO MANY WORDS
TO HELP PEOPLE FEEL
INCLUDED & SEEN.
WHAT A BEAUTIFUL
& PEACEFUL DEVELOPMENT,
LIKE THE DEVELOPMENT
OF THE HARP.

you'd think so.

But there are a lot
of people who feel burdened
by these extra letters;
there are some people who
even feel insulted by them.

Sometimes people will say,

In some ways, I can understand this complaint. It is a little bit of extra work, & it can be hard to keep up.

The reality of language is that it has to change & adapt in order to fit its changing & adapting people. As we move toward a world that can see, accept, & embrace all types of people, there need to be more words.

Nothing worthwhile in life ever stays the same.

My experience is overwhelmingly this:

When people feel truly seen, heard, known, & accepted, they don't need nearly as much personally.

They can get to work doing other important things in the world.

Is it so hard to see, hear, know, accept, & name all the gradients of sexuality?

It is not.

Just that little bit of extra work can be a deceptively big part of

shaking the world into place.

I, by the way, identify as

When I first heard what this word meant, it's hard to describe the magnitude of the flood of relief that followed.

I wonder: do you feel it when you read it now? It's this feeling of being all-of-a-sudden

not alone where you,

just moments before,

felt totally Other.

Anyway, babe, this is all to say: You're pansexual. You're attracted to women, men, & everyone in between. It will make your life awesome in the future. Love, Sophie

Chapter SIX:

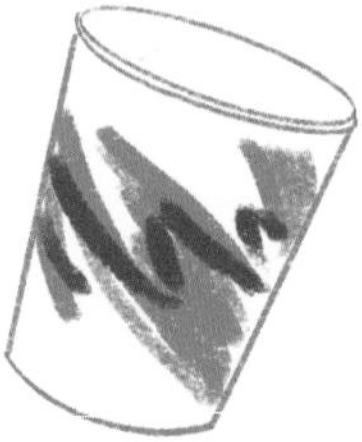

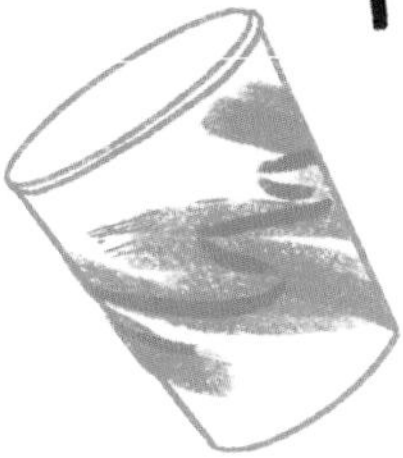

I Crumble a Lot

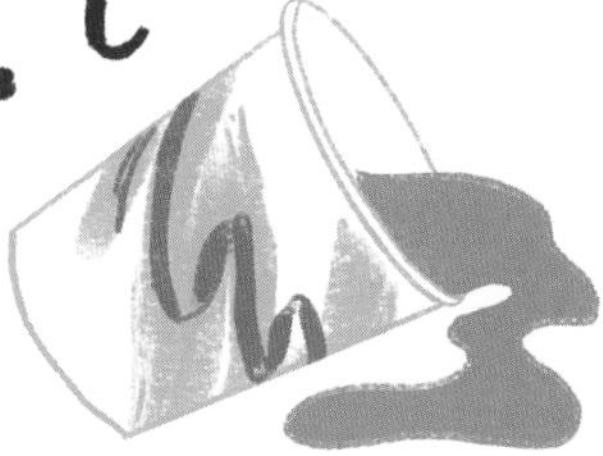

10/14/2001

Dear Diary,

God. I can never do anything right. I've been getting this overwhelming feeling of, "SOPHIE, YOU DO EVERYTHING WRONG, EVERYTHING BAD THAT EVER HAPPENS IS YOUR FAULT, AND I TRUST YOU WITH NOTHING!!!" from everyone. My mom especially, but with clubs and friends, too. I can't do anything right. I'm constantly told to be responsible for everything, and when I screw up I am royally criticized by everyone in the WHOLE FUCKING WORLD!

There just aren't enough hours in the day. "Sophie, do your homework. Sophie, read this.

Are you going to this protest? Can you organize this for me? Can you babysit on Friday? Can you help with this super important project? When can I see you again? Did you practice your piano today? You have a recital next week! Go to your yearbook pictures! Bake your cookies! I miss you and thus must inhabit every moment of your free time with my presence. Could you wear this on Valentine's Day? What are we doing for Swing Club today? Can I borrow your shoes? Can I borrow a dollar? Can I borrow another dollar since I lost the last one? I thought you were going to my concert! Todd's on the phone! You need to talk to Todd for the next hour since he lives in

Seattle and you never get to talk to him anymore! You look sick, you should be sleeping. Sophie, come out for track! We need you on the team! Your boyfriend is ugly! Now I'm depressed, let me vent to you. Sophie, what are you doing talking on a cell phone? I thought you were against those! I don't believe his parents are home, let me FUCKING CALL THEM 'CAUSE I DON'T TRUST you!!!

Love,
Sophie

11/18/2001

Dear Diary,

I feel so alone. Sometimes I think that if I write down all that's inside of me it will fill this empty spot I have. But it's still empty. Right now. If I could describe what it feels like, I would. It hurts! A real pain, not just a virtual one. It's an ache.

I feel so alone. I need someone who is there for me every day. And I really don't have that. No best friend, no boyfriend. I want to be in love, and I want someone I can talk to. The only comfort I can find is scrunching myself into myself so I'm sort of a ball. I try to squeeze my fat into my

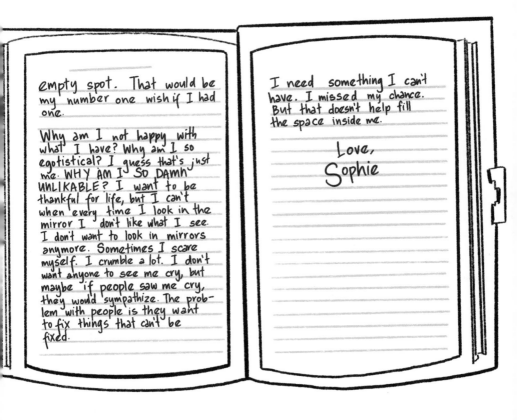

empty spot. That would be my number one wish if I had one.

Why am I not happy with what I have? Why am I so egotistical? I guess that's just me. WHY AM I SO DAMN UNLIKABLE? I want to be thankful for life, but I can't when every time I look in the mirror I don't like what I see. I don't want to look in mirrors anymore. Sometimes I scare myself. I crumble a lot. I don't want anyone to see me cry, but maybe if people saw me cry, they would sympathize. The problem with people is they want to fix things that can't be fixed.

I need something I can't have. I missed my chance. But that doesn't help fill the space inside me.

Love,

Sophie

Dear Sophie,

Wow. That _is_ a lot.

Did you ever think that all you really wanted (or maybe needed) was for someone to tell you that you were right, what you were going through _was_ a lot?

It's a small & simple thing that is hard to ask for: validation that you're not crazy for feeling like the world is crashing in all around you.

118

In the year 2020, I've been—most of the world has been—largely quarantined due to (try not to panic) a scary global pandemic no one saw coming. Because I've been quarantined, I've gotten to say no to a lot of things without feeling bad about it.

I just go,

SORRY! I CAN'T LEAVE MY HOUSE, IT'S A NATIONAL QUARANTINE, YOU UNDERSTAND.

Plenty of things have been canceled. Broadway plays we had tickets to, concerts, festivals, club meetings, birthday parties. With each subsequent cancellation, I've felt a jolt of pleasure & relief.

this is how people talk on the phone in 2020!!

AH, SO I MUST STAY HOME & DRAW PICTURES INSTEAD? ALRIGHT, FINE, IF I HAVE TO.

It has been a revelatory year. I've learned that it is possible for me to be calm & happy & consistently getting enough sleep & exercise;

I just have to cut most of the things in my life <u>out</u> of it.

But someone asked me recently if I thought that after quarantine I might say no to more things.

And I know I'm not going to.

You & I choose things like SWING CLUB & LOTS of FRIENDSHIPS & VOLUNTEERING & DUNGEON MASTERING

because we know they enrich our lives.

It will forever be nearly impossible to know our limits.

Over time, I got better at saying

no

to things.

Now I mostly only do things I really like. (I mean: Broadway plays!!! Birthday parties!!! Concerts!!! I can't complain.)

But it's true: there aren't enough hours in the day.

You & I are greedy for life.

& life is disorganized & messy & pretty universally a maximalist endeavor.

We have enormous privilege to enjoy the things we do, which means that it's doubly important to do things that are sometimes hard—like:

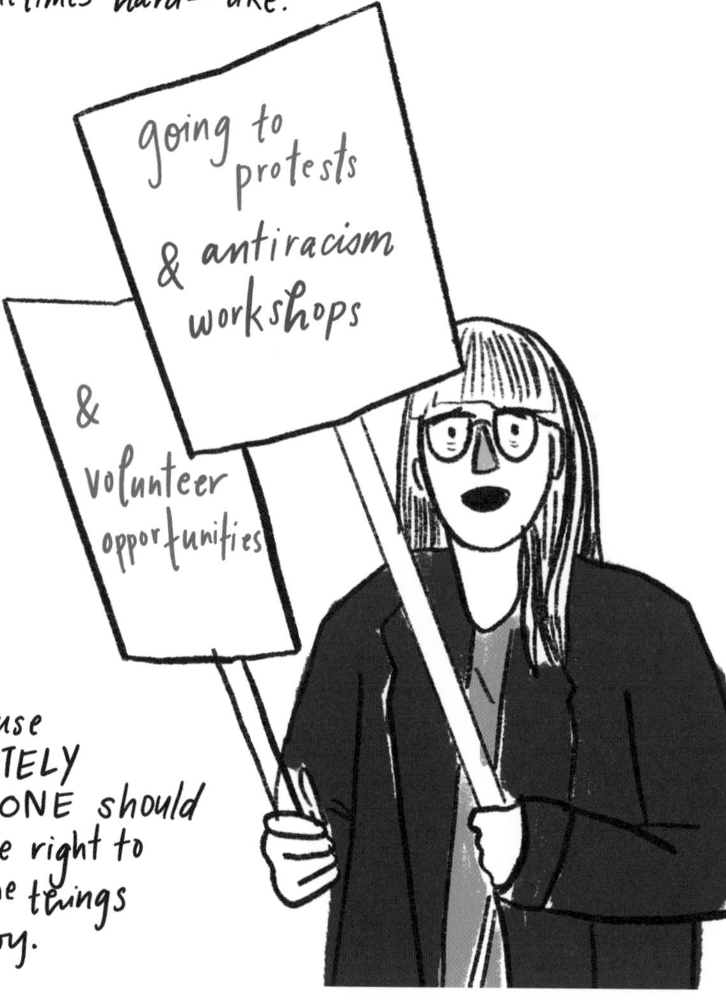
going to protests
& antiracism workshops
& volunteer opportunities

—because ABSOLUTELY EVERYONE should have the right to enjoy the things we enjoy.

And sometimes that becomes a juggling catastrophe waiting to happen.

123

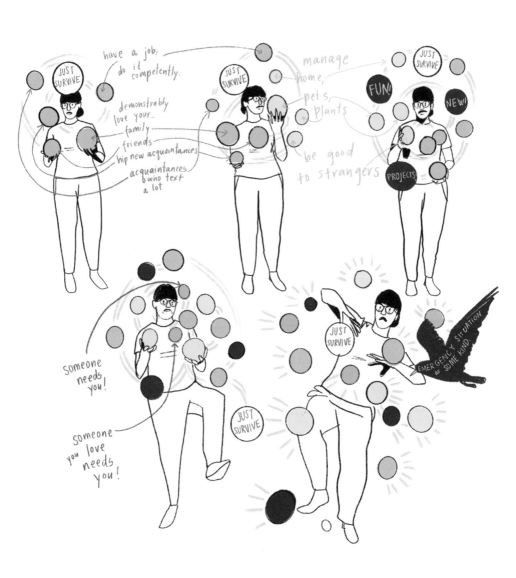

have a job,
do it competently.

JUST SURVIVE

demonstrably
love your...
family
friends
hip new acquaintances
acquaintances
who text
a lot

JUST SURVIVE

manage
home,
pets,
plants

be good
to strangers

JUST SURVIVE

FUN!

NEW!

PROJECTS!

Someone
needs
you!

Someone
you love
needs
you!

JUST SURVIVE

JUST SURVIVE

JUST SURVIVE

EMERGENCY SITUATION
OF SOME KIND.

124

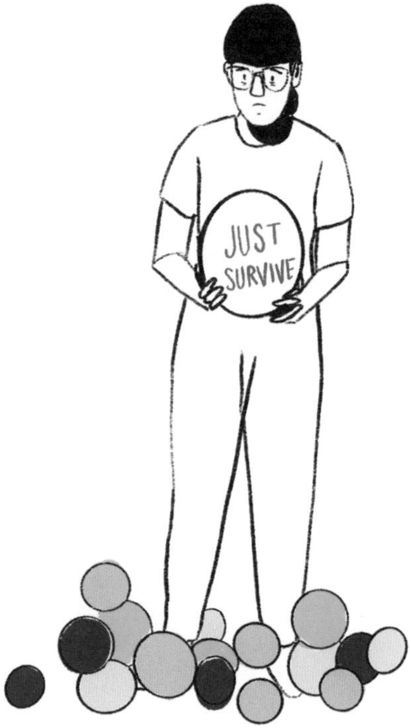
JUST
SURVIVE

But I guess I've come to realize,
That's just how it's going to be.

You can't figure everything out,
& occasionally the juggled things crash,
& that never feels good.

I wonder if giving in to this reality
might be a little bit freeing.

Maybe we can both
learn to take
ourselves slightly
less seriously.

Then we might
have time & energy
to both enjoy what is
great & fight for what
is right.

Love,

Sophie

2002, a panic attack feels like:

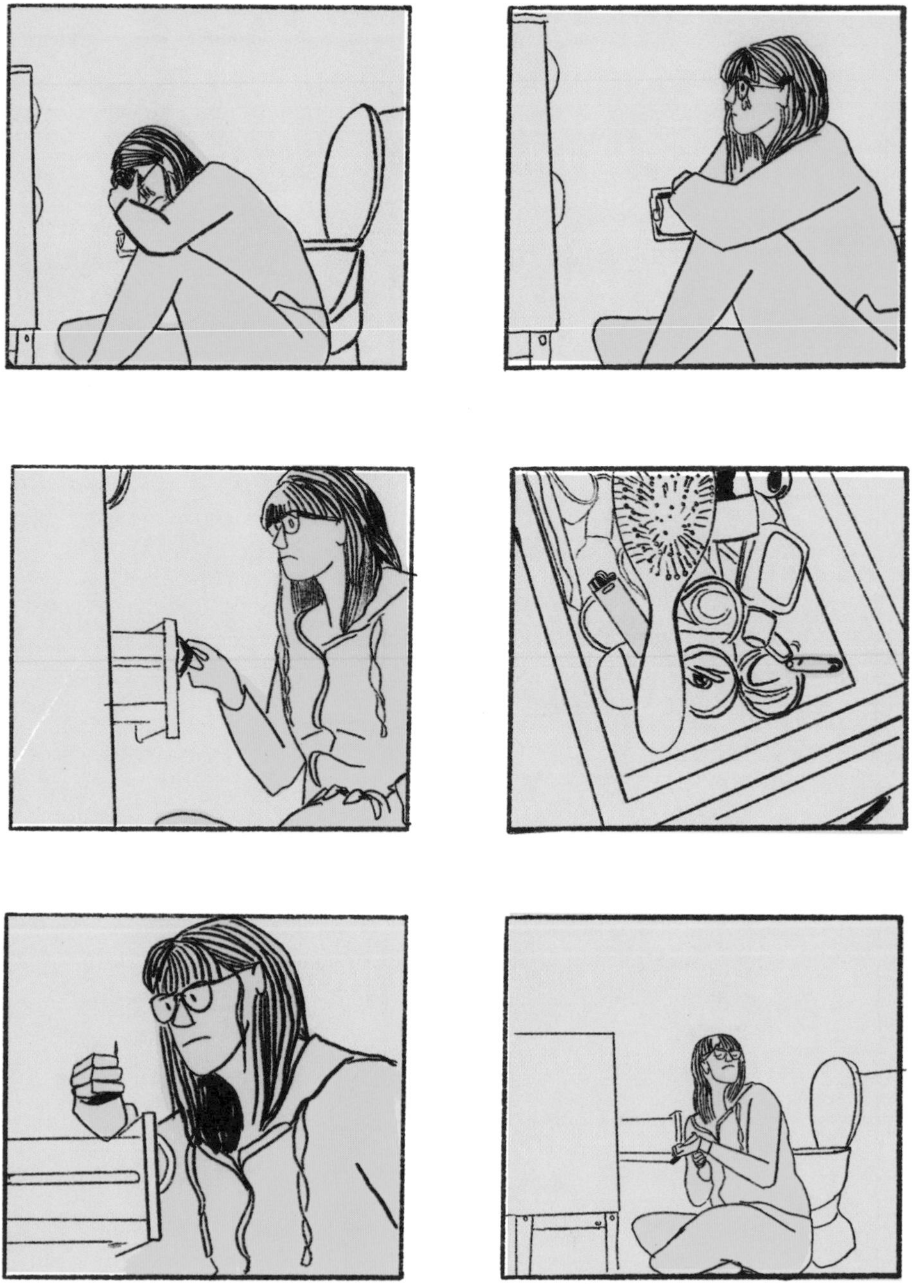

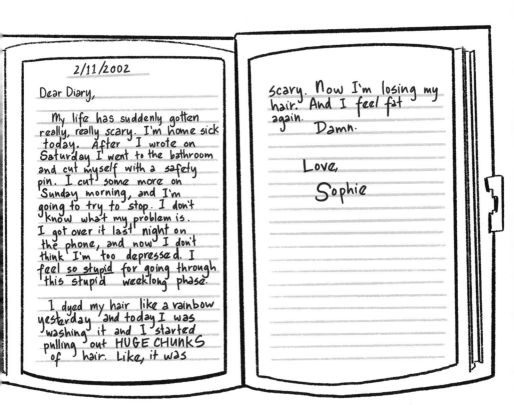

2/11/2002

Dear Diary,

My life has suddenly gotten really, really scary. I'm home sick today. After I wrote on Saturday I went to the bathroom and cut myself with a safety pin. I cut some more on Sunday morning, and I'm going to try to stop. I don't know what my problem is. I got over it last night on the phone, and now I don't think I'm too depressed. I feel so stupid for going through this stupid weeklong phase.

I dyed my hair like a rainbow yesterday and today I was washing it and I started pulling out HUGE CHUNKS of hair. Like, it was scary. Now I'm losing my hair. And I feel fat again.
Damn.

Love,

Sophie

Dear Sophie,

You were just trying to survive.

In fact, let me rephrase that slightly:

You were
SURVIVING.

You
SURVIVED.

You found a
soothing mechanism
that helped, &
you used it, &
now I am here, alive, writing back
to you —
because you took what
you needed.

I still cut myself. In truth, it's been about two years since I cut, but I can't be sure I'll never do it again.

Here are some things I don't believe are true about cutting:

① I don't believe people cut "just to get attention," as is often claimed. Although that word "just" bothers me. WHEN PEOPLE INDICATE THAT THEY NEED ATTENTION, & THEIR NEEDS AREN'T BEING MET, I'M NOT SURE WHAT'S WRONG WITH THAT.

② I don't believe cutting is shameful, or really any worse than smoking cigarettes, drinking alcohol, eating a bunch of sugar, or doing any of the other addictive things we human beings do to disassociate from painful feelings.

2A) Once, a therapist told me cutting was unique because

WHEN YOU CUT, YOU <u>know</u> YOU'RE HURTING YOURSELF, & THERE'S A PROBLEM WITH THAT.

Anyone who has ever been to middle school knows that when you smoke cigarettes you are hurting yourself. When I smoke a cigarette, the only difference for me is that with a cigarette I think, "THIS REALLY COULD KILL ME."

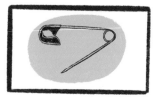

2B) I'm not condoning <u>any</u> of this behavior, by the way.

I'm saying it makes sense.

3) I don't think
cutting has to indicate to the
outside world that you're in pain,
or that you're choosing to hurt rather
than to act, or to get angry, or to do
something useful with your feelings.
I don't think cutting has to indicate
anything to anyone. It's not a
secret code for the rest of the
world to interpret.

Here's something I think is _wild_.
Trauma reactions—that's what you're experiencing
in these moments, by the way— are

PHYSICAL.

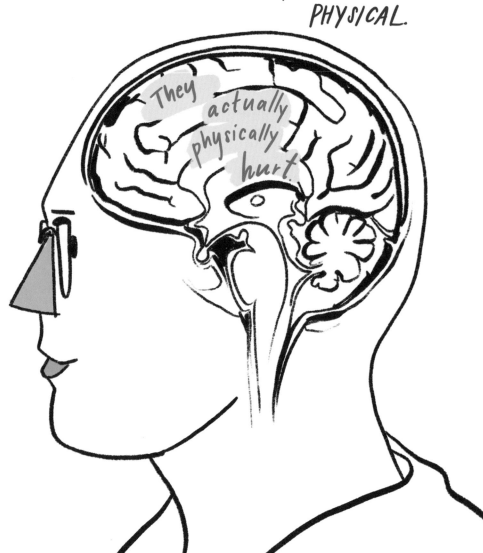

They actually physically hurt.

Sometimes I think such reactions probably feel a little like what it would feel like to be

MICROWAVED:

everything inside you BOILING & EXPLODING, without any indication on the surface.

For me, cutting felt like this:

The reason you cut & a lot of teenagers cut & I cut until recently is that we don't, as a society, make room for trauma responses to resolve themselves.

Healer & teacher & trauma therapist Resmaa Menakem has a series of steps in his book <u>MY GRANDMOTHER'S HANDS</u> he recommends for what to do when you feel that panicked, body-filling, annihilating, lizard-brain reaction coming up.

He calls them

the five anchors.

HERE THEY ARE:

1. soothe yourself to quiet your mind, calm your heart, & settle your body.

2. Simply notice the sensation, vibrations, & emotions in your body instead of reacting to them.

3. Accept the discomfort, & notice when it changes instead of trying to flee from it.

4. Stay present in your body as you move through the unfolding experience, with all its ambiguity & uncertainty, & respond from the best parts of yourself.

5. Safely discharge any energy that remains.

Over the last few months,
I've been practicing these.
Here is what I have learned:

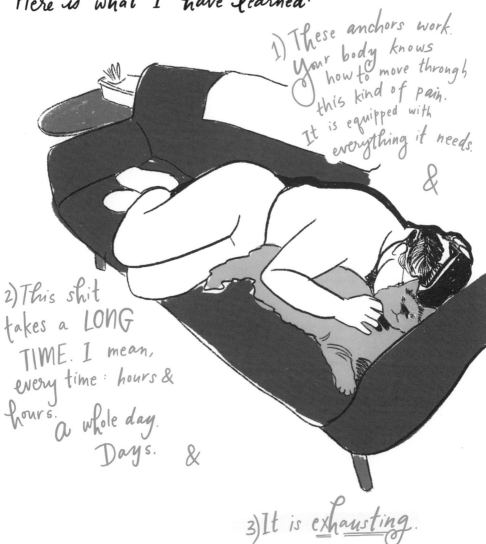

1) These anchors work.
Your body knows
how to move through
this kind of pain.
It is equipped with
everything it needs.

&

2) This shit
takes a LONG
TIME. I mean,
every time: hours &
hours.
A whole day.
Days. &

3) It is exhausting.

Yet the world wants us to move through our pain quickly. It wants us to solve our pain. It wants us to explain it, smoosh it, ignore it, or turn it into something else. Bodies are not designed to do that.

Other animals take the time they need to get through their brain responses.

They don't think,

WELL, I FEEL LIKE SHIT, BUT I'D BETTER PUSH MYSELF ANYWAY, BECAUSE THE WORLD DEMANDS THIS OF ME.

You, Sophie, are just one animal. But I can't blame you for thinking that you don't have time to feel the things you feel. The premium attached to productivity can feel impossible to unlearn.

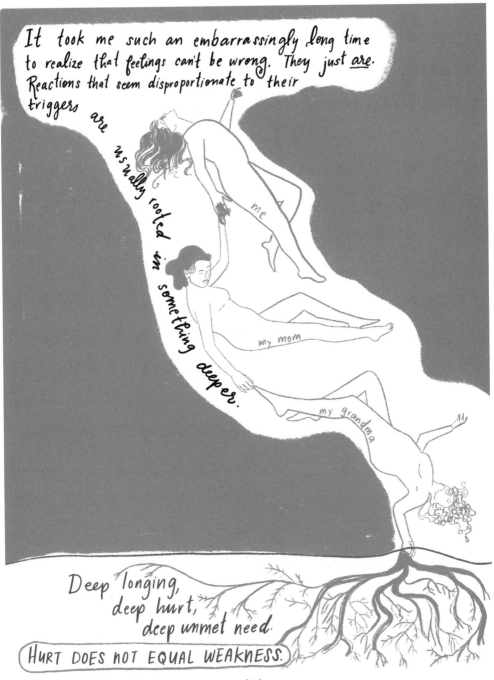

It took me such an embarrassingly long time to realize that feelings can't be wrong. They just _are_. Reactions that seem disproportionate to their triggers are usually rooted in something deeper.

me

my mom

my grandma

Deep longing,
deep hurt,
deep unmet need.

HURT DOES NOT EQUAL WEAKNESS.

Last week, my family was going through something hard. (It is not for me to tell you more about that, nor is it imperative to this story.) I felt The Feeling.

The one you're describing.

The "UH-OH, I WANT TO CUT MY SELF RIGHT _now_, WHERE IS A BATHROOM" feeling.

I was in the car going to the hardware store, & I felt myself crying; then I felt myself pushing back the crying.

My brain was going haywire, sending a bunch of different signals at once:

GO AHEAD! CRY! PANIC! THE WORLD IS ENDING!

& & &

PUSH THIS AWAY. THIS IS NOT THE TIME. FOCUS ON HARDWARE.

YOU CAN FIX THIS. SEND A BUNCH OF TEXT MESSAGES. CALL YOUR MOM. FIX IT. MAKE IT BETTER FOR EVERYONE ELSE, & THEN YOU'LL FEEL BETTER, TOO.

BY NOW, THIS IS ALL SO, SO FAMILIAR.

I parked the car &
turned my phone off.

It had started to rain.
I put my seat back &
closed my eyes & could hear
the rain doing its poetic thing
against the roof.

Out loud I said,

WHERE ARE
YOU FEELING THIS
IN YOUR BODY?

I felt it in my throat,
my neck, behind my eyes.

THAT'S INTERESTING

I thought.

I thought about the pain. It was like you
described: It really physically hurt! It ached.
There were moments where I felt like the pain would never
go
away.

On the other hand, the pain was changing:

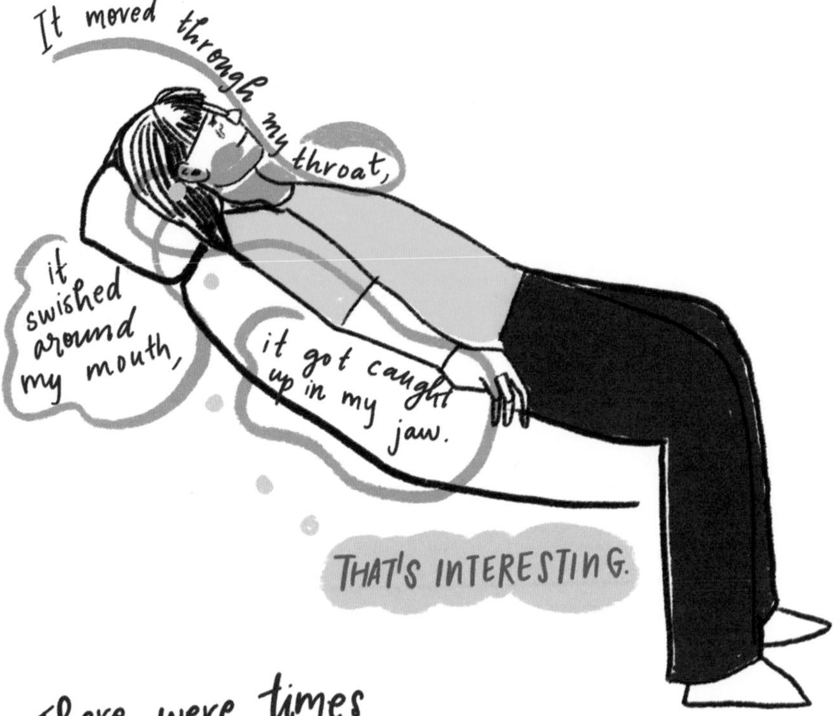

It moved through my throat,
it swished around my mouth,
it got caught up in my jaw.
THAT'S INTERESTING.

There were times my body wanted to

scream really loudly.

So I did!

There were times when my body wanted to

sob like the ocean.

I did.

For a whole hour, I sat there & felt it all.

And then, like a storm, the pain passed.

I felt _so_ tired.

The other thing I felt, Sophie, was proud.

I want to believe, & I want you to believe, that healing this kind of pain is possible. That we humans have the power to become our best animal selves, &, as Menakem puts it, "metabolize our trauma." I am not sure. I am a beginner trying out new things to deal with old hurt. I have also tried:

meditation,

holistic diets,

exercise,

lots & lots & LOTS & LOTS of therapy,

yoga,

Wellbutrin,

walks in the woods,

& even pot!

(SORRY NOT SORRY, SOPH; WE HAVE TO DO OUR BEST WITH WHAT WE HAVE.)

Some things work better than other things.

146

At one of my readings one time, a lady raised her hand & asked,

YOU SAY IN YOUR BOOK YOU STRUGGLE WITH MENTAL HEALTH ISSUES. WHY?

UHHH, I ... I ... UHHHHHHHH

I wish I had said,

BECAUSE, PROBABLY MILLENNIA AGO, ONE HUMAN BEING HURT ANOTHER HUMAN BEING, & THE HURT HUMAN'S PREFRONTAL CORTEX WAS CONFUSED & DIDN'T FULLY PROCESS WHAT IT WAS GOING THROUGH, SINCE EMOTIONAL HURT IS SO WEIRD & DIFFICULT TO DIGEST. AND SO SHE HURT ANOTHER HUMAN, BECAUSE UNHEALED HURT BEGETS HURT, & THAT HUMAN HURT ANOTHER HUMAN, & SOON THERE WERE GENERATIONS OF HUMANS HURTING EACH OTHER LEFT & RIGHT, CAUSING EACH OTHER TRAUMA & NOT EVER DEALING WITH IT OR HEALING FROM IT. & THIS HAPPENED & HAPPENED & HAPPENED RIGHT UP UNTIL MY PARENTS WERE BORN, & THEY GOT HURT, & SO THEY HURT ME, & ALL THE PEOPLE AROUND ME—MY CLASSMATES & TEACHERS & FRIENDS & FOES—WERE ALL ALSO SIMULTANEOUSLY FEELING HURT & ACTING OUT HURT AS A RESULT, & BEFORE YOU KNOW IT, I REALIZED I HAD SOME MENTAL HEALTH ISSUES!

But instead I said,

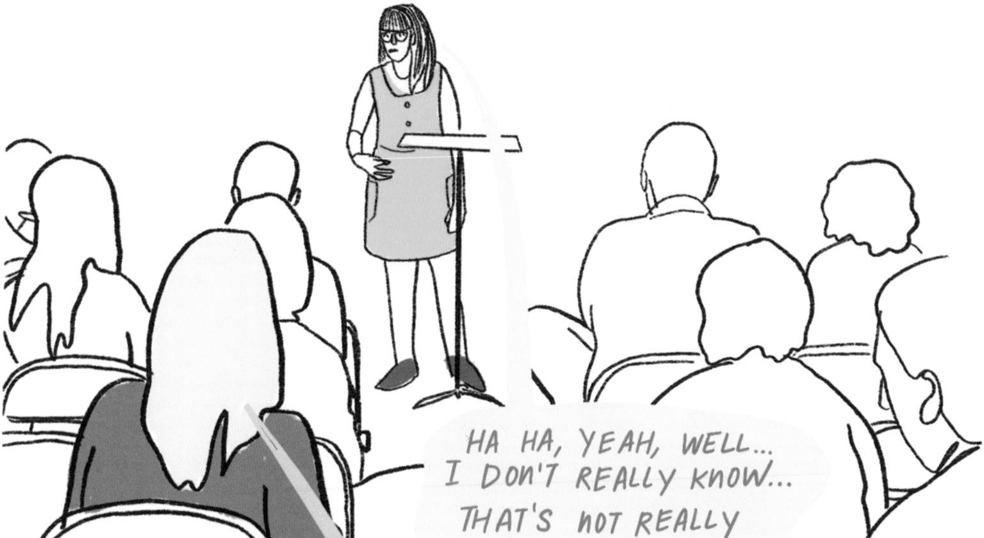
HA HA, YEAH, WELL... I DON'T REALLY KNOW... THAT'S NOT REALLY WHAT THE BOOK'S ABOUT.
WELL THEN WHY DID YOU PUT IT IN THE BOOK?

And the answer is that I am not a full story without the parts that hurt.

Sophie, you did what you needed to do to survive. I'm still doing what I need to do to survive, & learning as I go.

I'm proud of both of us.
Love,
Sophie

PS. Re: hair falling out. Eat. Please eat food. When you don't eat food, your hair falls out.

chapter SEVEN:

Alexis Is Bugging The Hell Out of Me!

1/1/2001

Dear Diary,

I am at the beach and UGH Alexis is bugging the hell out of me! I wish she would realize that I AM FRIGGIN' OLDER THAN SHE is! She always acts like my mom or a policeman or something. Whenever she sees me doing anything that is remotely wrong she blows up at me like I'm some bank robber felon or something. "WHAT THE HECK!?" Just today I found a note that said: "Hem hem? Why're there pieces of cotton clinging to your bra and a huge wad of it in our suitcase? I'm on to you..."

Yeah, so, I stuff my bra! It's not such a huge sin! It's not like I'm hurting anyone! It's not my fault that my boobs are smaller than hers are! I need a little support so that at least my fat looks evenly distributed. I don't tell her because she makes fun of me to my face all the time (when I told her before) and because she'd probably tell my friends (she's done THAT before too) and because every time she'd see me sneak a snippet of cotton into my bra, she'd raise her eyebrows and shamefully turn away.

Guess what else I do that's such a moral sin?

151

I masturbate. Omigosh, like half the population doesn't. She just doesn't realize that it's not such a huge deal. But, because I do this terrible deed, Alexis has deduced that all my things are "slimy," or "have been between my thighs" or something terrible like that. She will also make fun of me for that.

Once someone told me I was gross for wearing the same bra every day. Embarrassed out of my mind, I told them that I had three of the same bra. A white lie. Well, once Zoe brought it up while Alexis was around and Alexis popped

my lie and laughed about it. Zoe hasn't trusted me since.

And last but not least, she throws these anger fits. She will shout SO LOUD if someone even mentions something in a teasing manner or doesn't agree with her. She would scream in a debate, she would shout in an argument. So much for soft voicing. I wish she would just calm down and take things easy, step by step, quietly sorting things out. Ugh.

Love,

Sophie

Dear Sophie,

Alexis, your sister,

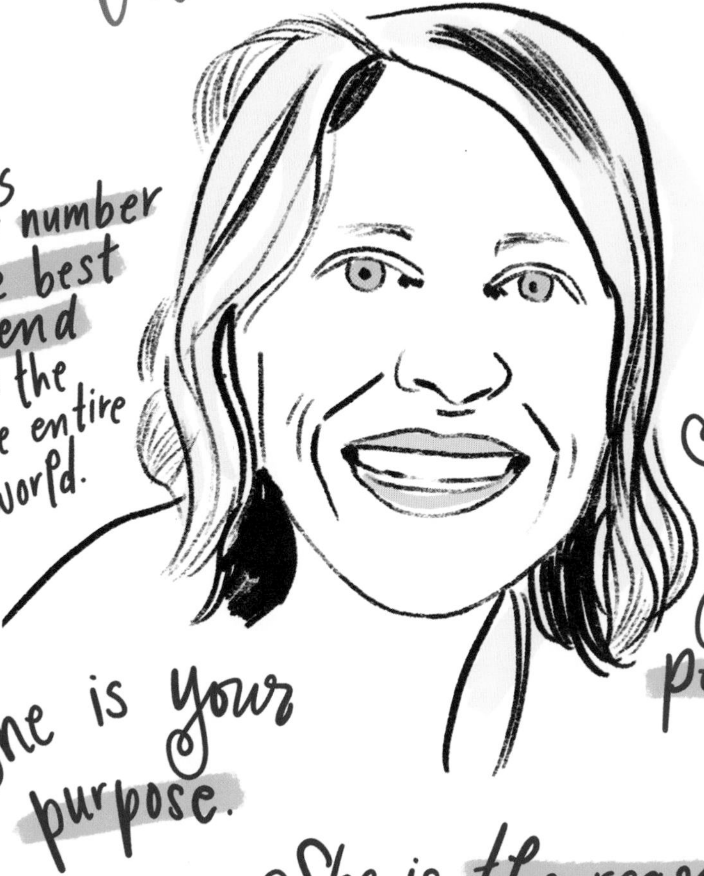

is your number one best friend in the whole entire world.

She is your person.

She is your purpose.

She is the reason you wake up each day & go to bed each night.

Alexis & I once lived in the same house after college. Twice she moved across the country to live where I lived.

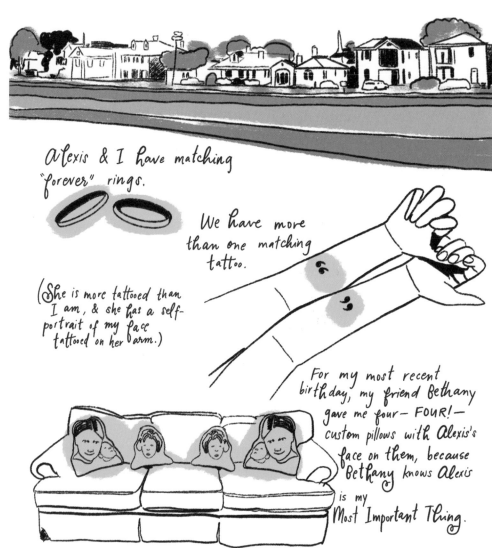

Alexis & I have matching "forever" rings.

We have more than one matching tattoo.

(She is more tattooed than I am, & she has a self-portrait of my face tattooed on her arm.)

For my most recent birthday, my friend Bethany gave me four — FOUR! — custom pillows with Alexis's face on them, because Bethany knows Alexis is my Most Important Thing.

Six months ago, I flew to Portland to watch Alexis give birth. Did I actually watch it? I _did_. I was uncomfortably wedged in a corner while, like, 8 nurses flitted around Alexis, holding her various body parts & giving her directions while they waited for the doctor to get there.

Things were happening really fast. One nurse said to me,

HERE, COULD YOU PLUG THIS IN?

And she handed me a plug, & I've never been happier to have something to plug in in all my life. I don't even know _what_ I plugged in. I only know that those were the only 23 seconds of the entire labor where I knew what to do, & where I wasn't staring at my sister's vagina.

It's obvious to me now why people shouldn't try to write about birth: it's bigger than language. The only other thing like that is death.

How appropriately symmetrical.

156

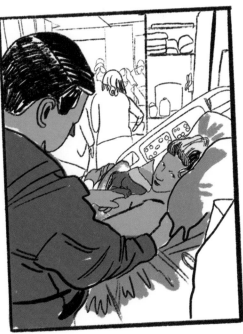

Alexis had a late pregnancy & a fast labor. She screamed. Her baby looked like a gray liver when it came out, & then it became a he, & then he was pink & also screaming. At that point, I took as many pictures as I thought possible, because this, like the plug, was another job for me to do, & I really, really wanted a job. Later, we ate Thai food (I also got to pick up the Thai food!) that was simultaneously just mediocre & the best food anyone in the hospital room that night had ever eaten.

I tell you all this because

NONE OF THIS BUSINESS about bra stuffing & bra rewearing & masturbating & even the anger really matters. You got one sister in this life, & she has also been your mother & your daughter & your best friend & your girlfriend & your ally & your enemy & every other thing a person can be to another person.

Those are the only things that matter at all.

All that said: this was bullshit and Alexis was totally wrong & you were right. Bra stuffing is industrious; masturbation is one of the best things about being alive; & you shouldn't have lied about having three of the same bras, but I get it.

Boooo, Alexis.
Boo.

Love,
Sophie

PS—Let us hope —HOPE!—That way more than half the population masturbates. Let us hope that Alexis is privately included.

chapter

EIGHT:

Today Was
Greatly Significant
in the History
of
America

1/22/1999

Dear Diary,

Sorry I haven't been writing. I got pretty sick last week and stayed home for four days. We're studying WW Ⅱ in class. It's worth mega tears. I'm way serious.

I've been thinking: why do people like me? I'm just wondering. I feel like I've wasted 2 years as a fat loser. Of course people want to be my friend! I'm nothing to compete with! I always look so bad in pictures. I can't get them right, you know? One day, a pic will come out well. But why not today diary? Why not? 160 pounds. I'm serious. I'm not changing. I want to! Honestly! No one will ever ask me out

otherwise. Huh. No one will ever, ever look at me as a GIRL. It's like this guy looks at a picture of all the girls in my school. Say he desperately needs a date. Say every girl with a boyfriend is Xed out. Say every girl is Xed out. And I'd stand out like a bright red tulip in a patch of white ones. No, I'm not pretty enough to be considered a tulip. Like one fat elephant in a field of daisies and he'd probably transfer schools before asking me out. I don't blame him.

We go out to the tulip farm every year and I'm always the one at the snack booth.

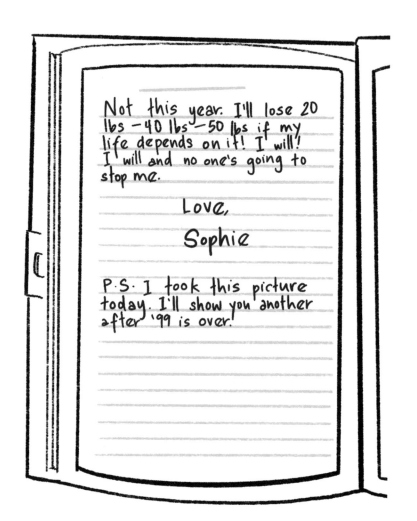

Not this year. I'll lose 20 lbs — 40 lbs — 50 lbs if my life depends on it! I will! I will and no one's going to stop me.

Love,

Sophie

P.S. I took this picture today. I'll show you another after '99 is over!

Dear Sophie,

Whoooooa, ok. We really switched gears there after "WWII was bad," huh? I mean, yeah, good to acknowledge that throughout history, there's been real pain & suffering. But as a reader, I'm unconvinced you actually cried "mega tears" over WWII. But okay, let's cut you some slack. You're young! You're mostly not thinking about WWII. THAT'S NORMAL!

WWII: A HISTORY

OFFICIAL TEAR-JERKER

I am looking at this *fabulous* enclosed Polaroid of you in an awesome leopard-print underwear set & I'm thinking,

BEFORE

"THIS GIRL LOOKS GREAT! WHAT IS SHE TALKING ABOUT?!"

The thing that is so **difficult** about this state of being for you is that you can't see any of the things that <u>really</u> <u>matter</u> about the human that you are. And I get it. First, you don't yet have the perspective that comes with life experience. Also, trust me: you never fully unlearn the **inane** message that something is wrong with your body. But let's look at the facts:

*You just wrote a great
sentence about being a
red tulip in a patch
of white ones. That's a cliché,
but you don't know that, having
never heard it before; you just
saw a field of white tulips with
a random red one in it & thought,

HUH. THAT'S
SOMETHING
TO NOTICE.

You noticed it
because you're a
WRITER.

COOL!

* You have a freaking Polaroid camera! <u>With</u> film <u>in</u> <u>it</u>! Do you know how <u>rare</u> that is?

* Your love of snacks is an asset.

*You are so sensitive & thoughtful. Look! You even apologize to your DIARY for neglecting it.

You go out of your way to see things from other people's perspectives. I appreciate that about you.

What I'm noticing is how you are dwelling on realities that—no matter how determined you may be— you cannot change. I say you cannot change these realities because—I hate to break it to you—there's no amount of weight that you could lose that would make you feel good enough. That's an impossible-to-achieve standard, & whether or not you know it, pretty much all the girls in your grade—even the really, really skinny ones— are stressing out over this, too.

But there are lots of things you can change! Even at your age, you can use your privilege for good. And now it's time to tell you a little about what I've learned about privilege, because with some perspective on that, you have the capacity to be a major force for good in the world.

In almost all ways, you are a member of the DOMINANT SOCIAL GROUP.*

For instance!

YOU ARE WHITE

YOU ARE ABLE-BODIED

YOUR PARENTS EARN ABOVE THE POVERTY LINE, & YOU GET AN ALLOWANCE

AT THIS POINT IN TIME YOU'RE STILL CHRISTIAN (CATHOLIC VERSION, BUT WHO'S PAYING ATTENTION?)

*a.k.a.— THE GROUP IN SOCIETY THAT CONTROLS THE VALUE SYSTEM & REWARDS WITHIN THAT SOCIETY

It's true that you're a girl, & it's true that you're pansexual, & those are sometimes difficult things to be.

I'm still learning about my privilege. Every time I go to a daylong (or weeklong!) workshop about antiracism or white supremacy, I learn so many new things they can't all fit in my brain.

I leave with discomfort & unanswered questions.

168

It's important to sometimes be uncomfortable.
I can't fix everything that's wrong with the
world, & I get things wrong
so, so,
<u>so</u> much of the time.
This is exactly why it matters so much to keep showing up.

Some of the work is about learning.

Some of the work is about
internally
healing &
<u>UN</u>learning.

Some of the work is about going out & doing.

None of the work is ever over, & it is your responsibility
to show up for it. Every. Damn. Day.   OK?

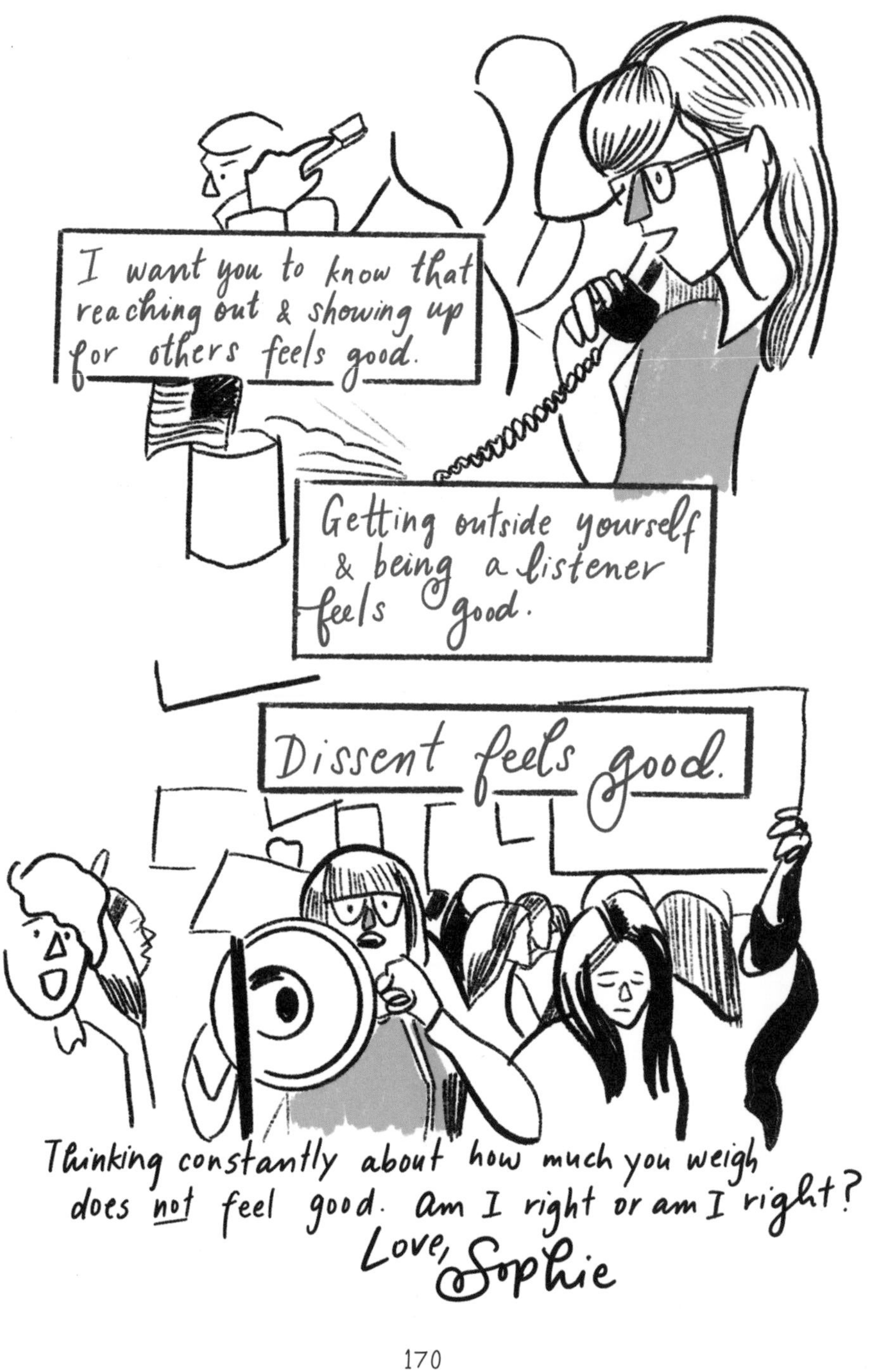

I want you to know that reaching out & showing up for others feels good.
Getting outside yourself & being a listener feels good.
Dissent feels good.
Thinking constantly about how much you weigh does not feel good. Am I right or am I right?
Love, Sophie

9/11/2001

Dear Diary,

Today was greatly significant in the history of America. Around sometime this morning a plane flew into the World Trade Center. Then another one... right into the other side. Can you believe it? It was unbelievable. The Pentagon was the next target. About 10,000 people died! 10,000 people!!! That could have been me or my mom. My mom used to work there. On the 50th floor. All those people are gone. Families all over the world are in mourning. We might go to war. I just can't believe it. This is bigger than anything that's happened in my lifetime. Eerie. Scary. Momentous.

But I have something about my life I have to update you about. On Saturday I went to the callbacks for the theatre group Teens NW. I really hope I get it, it would be unbelievably fun. I also met the cutest guy ever. His name was Eli. He's a sophomore at a private school. He's got this blonde hair and this great sense of style. He is amazing. I want to hug and kiss him all night.

And now I'm actually over Trevor.

Swing Dancing Club's gonna be so awesome at school this year.

Love,
Sophie

Dear
Sophie,

When you are young, everything is a big deal, &
it's hard to tell if something is a bigger deal than anything else. I
remember how it was hard to tell how big a deal 9/11 was.
Even when you thought 10,000 people had died
(IN FACT, IT WAS SLIGHTLY FEWER THAN 3,000,
A TERRIBLE, TRAGIC NUMBER ALL THE SAME),
you were not sure exactly
how big a deal this was.

But you suspected.

And so you knew, even though all you could think
about was Eli & Trevor & how you had a new crush
& Swing Dancing Club, you should probably cover your
bases & write about 9/11.

And this entry was what
you wrote.

As I write this, the year is 2021, &, as
I've mentioned, I teach writing to
high school kids. I also mentioned the
worldwide pandemic, which is a big deal, too.
It's a big deal in a way that nothing has been a big deal
since 9/11 — which is saying something because

(major spoilers ahead)

there have been hurricanes & wars & so, so many
mass shootings. There's been global climate change,
which has meant fires, floods, polar vortexes, tornadoes,
& mosquitoes taking over.

But nothing has washed over everything
the way the global pandemic has.

I told my students that they should

WRITE SOMETHING DOWN EVERY DAY.

They are seniors in high school, & now, because of this virus, they are part of history.

But historians don't need you to write about the facts of what happened — they have news reports for that; they want to know about how people feel, & what they do every day. That's the stuff that the newspapers will never be able to all the way g̲e̲t̲. When I write in my diary now about how it feels to be in a global pandemic, a lot of it is sort of boring minutiae, but it's the kind of stuff I wish yo̲u̲'̲d̲ written after the world changed completely for ̲y̲o̲u̲.

Like, I remember you went to this theater rehearsal the night that George W. Bush insinuated that there would be a war. The guys in charge said

IF YOU'RE GOING TO DO THEATRE, YOU CAN'T CARE ABOUT WHAT'S GOING ON IN THE WORLD BECAUSE IT'S YOUR JOB TO TAKE PEOPLE AWAY FROM ALL THAT.

You felt crushed & betrayed. You didn't eat dinner.

But I appreciate that you left this entry for me. There's more in what you <u>didn't</u> write than there is in what you wrote.

You didn't write how you weren't sure how scared you were supposed to be.

You didn't write that two of your teachers cried.

You didn't write that a boy in your biology class had said something about how America needed to keep Muslims out, & you knew that that was wrong, but you didn't say anything.

Me & Jess & Toby! Fun timezzz.

The girl who didn't write those things wasn't sure what to do.

She was <u>performing</u>.

She was acting like a 16-year-old who went through a major world event, who didn't know what to say about it & didn't know what to feel.

Ooh lah lah, Ben!

Fam portrait, XMAS, 2001!

I wonder if this is something I still do; & if it is, I wonder why.

Love, Sophie

chapter NINE:

Lists of Things I Like

8/12/2000

Dear Diary,

Happiness is good! Here are some things that make me happy:

FRUITY
MENTOS

KITES

NAIL
POLISH

WEIRD
AL

JARS OF
INK

MOVIES
WITH
TWIZZLERS

WEIRD AL'S
BLACK PANTS

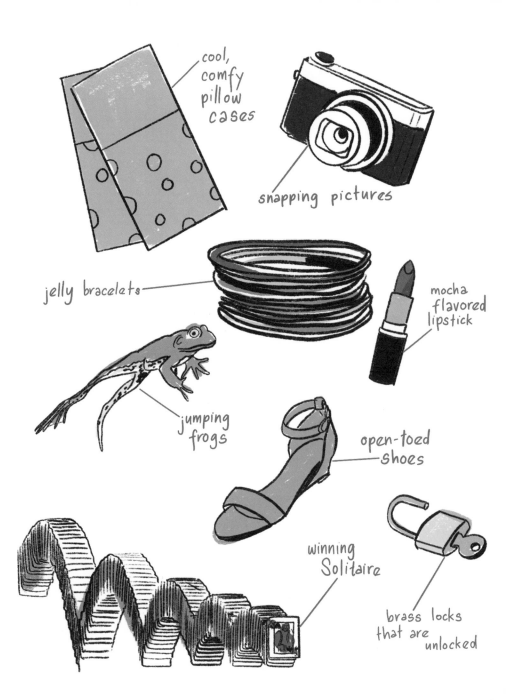

cool, comfy pillow cases

snapping pictures

jelly bracelets

mocha flavored lipstick

jumping frogs

open-toed shoes

winning Solitaire

brass locks that are unlocked

white white teeth

genuine smiles

CREAM C[heese]

movies that make me cry (a.k.a. "Bed of Roses")

large piles of cream cheese

bizarre magazines

CATFANCY 1913

MASSAGE YOUR CAT

BED OF ROSES

stand-up comedy on Comedy Central

mocha almond fudge ice cream

7/3/2001
Dear Diary,
Here is a list of fabulous things:

Hot
bumbleberry
pie

red sneakers

Marilyn Monroe movies
in the afternoon

air-tight packets
of dried fruit

Rider Strong
(sigh)

good finds
at thrift
stores

TIME-0

"Empire Records"

vegan
pizza
dough

amusing post cards

POSTCARD

EGGY!

the smell of
Joe's deodorant

lying in the
shade, staring
at the earth
on a sunny
day

writing an amazing song

182

perfectly fitting jeans

melty Popsicles

Halloween

the blue flavor of Top Ramen

Top Ramen

old home movies

undeveloped film— when you turn it in to be developed

200

knowing you look good

elephant ears

TBS SUPERSTATION

when a movie you want to see airs on Superstation

日本語

having an entire conversation in Japanese

vegan cookies that taste good

dogwood trees

walking somewhere aimlessly and ending up somewhere new

rounding lap 12

multitudes of buttercups

184

a song that evokes vivid memories

an overstretched shirt shrinking perfectly in the wash

finding a great new word in the dictionary

DICTIONARY

lint balls

finding something small that you lost

little, tiny spiders

plump raspberries

reading old diaries (Future Sophie, you're hot!)

VCRS you can understand

(Quick side note from 2021: Thanks, Young Sophie! You too!)

Chapter TEN:

I Don't Understand

6/27/2001

Dear Diary,

What if everything you're depending on... like, everything... doesn't pull through? What if you believe in something so much that when you start to realize it isn't true, you're pretty much screwed? If that little building block sort of just crashes to the ground? Like if you know you're going to Europe this summer, but suddenly you can't afford it so you have to plan your whole summer over again? What if it was like that, but it affected your entire life? Like you build your entire existence around a "fact" that wasn't actually factual at all? Like you thought you would... I don't know, have a kid, and then you discover that it's impossible to have a child due to some sort of defect. And you had planned to be a stay-at-home mom and run a daycare for your kid, and all of a sudden that's just ruined, just like that?

Like what if I don't get to perform when I grow up? My whole life would be so different than I am planning it. I plan to sing! To meet a perfect husband on the stage, to be someone. What, though, what if something better suddenly came along, or something *almost* as good? Do I give up my dream? Do I abandon my life for this NEW thing? How do I know what I'm going to be and where I'm going to go? How do I choose? Is there really a

187

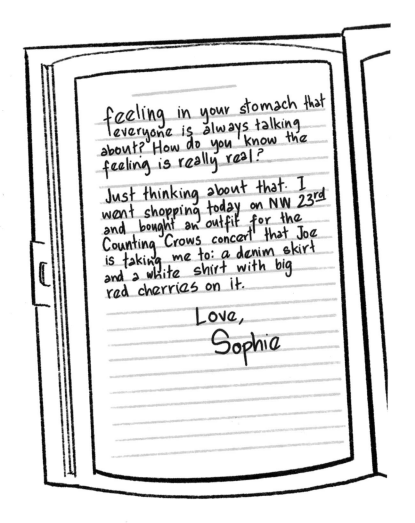

feeling in your stomach that everyone is always talking about? How do you know the feeling is really real?

Just thinking about that. I went shopping today on NW 23rd and bought an outfit for the Counting Crows concert that Joe is taking me to: a denim skirt and a white shirt with big red cherries on it.

Love,

Sophie

Dear Sophie,
I have to commend your relatively young understanding of the proper usage of

AFFECT & EFFECT

Very few of my older students have mastered that grammar rule— and they're <u>IN COLLEGE</u>.

(For the record, & so you stay sharp, other things young adults of the future can't get right include: "lay & lie"; excessively ending sentences with prepositions; overusing the word "very".)

So, yes, as I have stated throughout our correspendence: I'm a teacher!

I wanted to be a performer for fifteen years,

& I am a teacher.

The bottom line is that most people who dream of being performers do not exactly get to be performers.

But before you get existential & snot-cry all over your brand-new cherry shirt, let me tell you:

190

There isn't a thing I would change.
I don't want to spoil too many things
for you — because

part of what's so lovely is watching the wonderful stuff

bloom before you in slow motion —

but being a grown-up

is actually GREAT.

Even as you age out of being the next Gwen Stefani (JUST SO YOU KNOW, GWEN WILL NEVER GET ANY OLDER BECAUSE IT TURNS OUT SHE IS PROBABLY AN ALIEN),

things continue to be GREAT.

Teaching IS performing!

Your audience is smaller than Gwen's, but your students get so much more from you than a stadium of fair-weather fans.

Your act is more multifaceted than you could have imagined:

YOU TELL JOKES.

You PERFORM MONOLOGUES.

you present FILMS.

You DISPENSE ADVICE.

But the main things you get to do as a teacher are _listen_ & _hear_.

I mean "hear" in a deep way that you won't understand right now, because the ability to listen to & truly hear other humans is what differentiates a

child

from an

adult,

& you're not an adult yet.

Which is how it should be. Be a child as long as you need.

This sounds like an after-school special, but I swear it's true:

LISTENING TO OTHER PEOPLE IS A GREAT DEAL MORE INTERESTING, FULFILLING, & INVIGORATING THAN GETTING OTHER PEOPLE TO LISTEN TO YOU.

As human beings, we belong to each other.

In the *future*, this gets even harder to believe.

(Crazily, the internet becomes a massive instrument of <u>dis</u>connection. I know! Tell that to your <u>MODEM</u>, am I right?)

Sometimes, you'll remember.

You'll go to a peace rally & everyone will start singing with one voice;

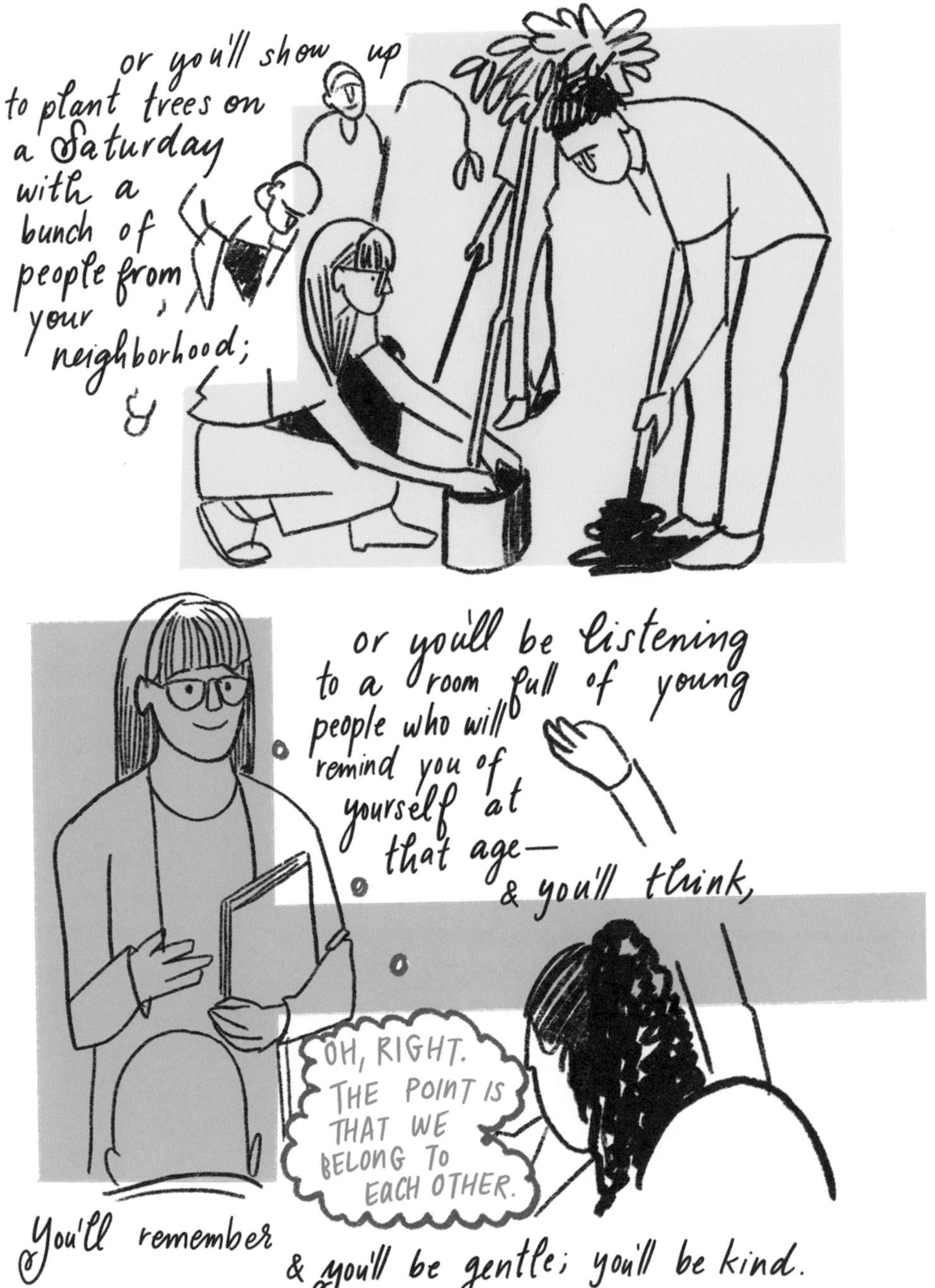
or you'll show up to plant trees on a Saturday with a bunch of people from your neighborhood;
&
or you'll be listening to a room full of young people who will remind you of yourself at that age—
& you'll think,
OH, RIGHT. THE POINT IS THAT WE BELONG TO EACH OTHER.
You'll remember
& you'll be gentle; you'll be kind.

And really, you could do anything with your life—

you could
train
dolphins

or crunch
numbers

or harvest
carrots or
whatever—

& as long as you remember that tenet of connection,
life will feel, at least pretty often,
full & interesting & just & right.

Pit-of-your-stomach right.
Have fun at the concert!
Love, Sophie

4/22/2001

Dear Diary,

Why am I not happy? I don't get it. Ughghghhhgh. Why do I feel unhappy? God gave me so much. I simply am sad. I know I'll eventually get out of this slump, because I always do. I never stay forever sad, I just change things around and I'm really happy again and I don't know why I was ever sad. I just don't know what I want to fix. I feel so uneasy about myself. I want to just crawl into myself and not come out for a very long time. I want to be alone for a while and not be so concerned about pleasing everyone. I want to please myself right now. But that's selfish! I'm selfish. And I'm so jealous all the time.

Whenever people do things without me, it makes me feel like I want to cry, even if I don't. And I can't tell anyone. I CAN'T be this selfish! Oh, I'm so confused! I don't even know what I want anymore. Help! Why am I such a wreck? When will I be able to gather up the pieces and move on from this pathetic little period I don't understand? Sometimes I THINK writing this out will help, but it never does.

Love,
Sophie

Dear Sophie,

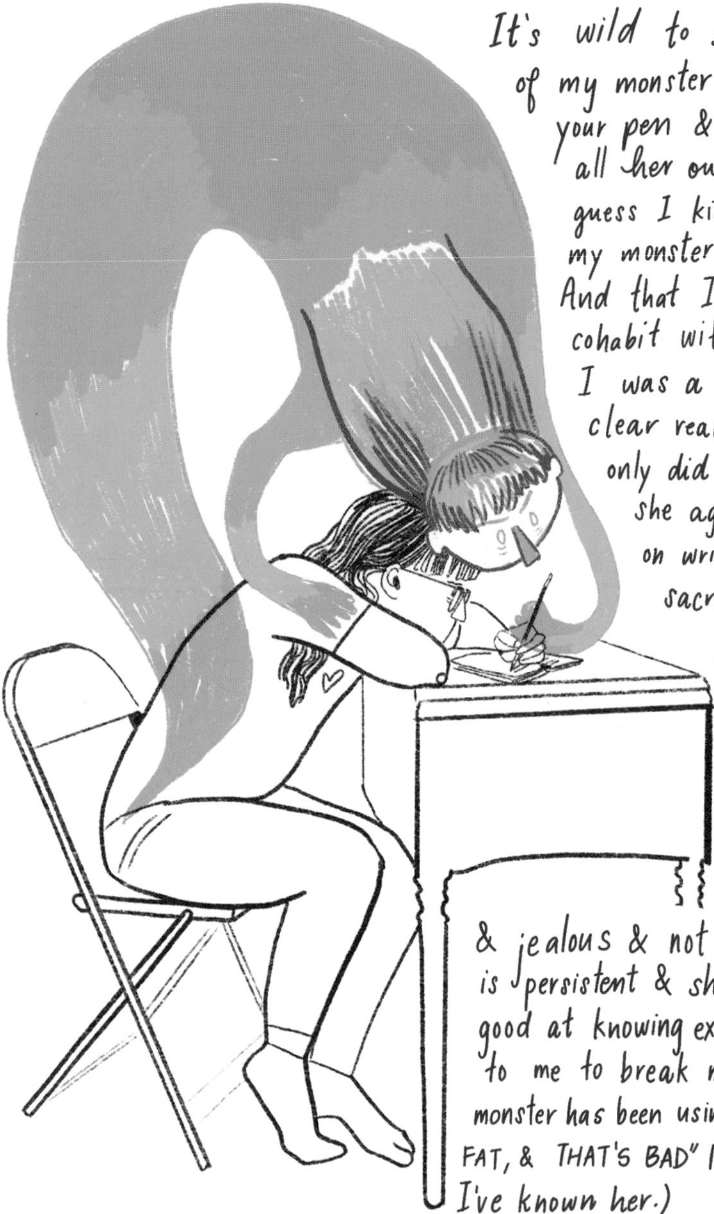

It's wild to see evidence of my monster taking over your pen & writing down all her own thoughts. I guess I kind of thought my monster was new-ish? And that I didn't have to cohabit with her when I was a child? But it's clear reading this that not only did we share space, she aggressively insisted on writing in your own, sacred diary.

"MY MONSTER" is what I now call that voice that says all those mean things about being selfish & jealous & not good enough. She is persistent & she's very good at knowing exactly what to say to me to break my heart. (My monster has been using that whole, "YOU'RE FAT, & THAT'S BAD" line for as long as I've known her.)

I know it seems like this monster is a total bitch, & sure, you can think that.

For most of the years I've been alive, I've thought this monster was the enemy.

But now I'm not so sure.

Last year, my best friend broke up with me. I was the saddest I've been in recent memory. My monster came back with a zeal I had not known she could have. She followed me around EVERYWHERE. Yes, even INTO THE BATHROOM to tell me I was

NOT PEEING RIGHT!!!

(SHE DID SEEM TRULY BITCHY AT THAT TIME.)

I felt smothered.

So I sat in the yard & decided I would write a letter to my monster.

As I wrote, the monster started to respond.

Even you, a fairly spiritual woo-adjacent teenager will find this whole "communicating with one's monster" thing to be... a bit much. But hand to God — it helped.

I wrote to the monster, & she wrote back,

Sophie, you lie all the time. You have to stop lying.

203

Everyone lies.
  You've rationalized the lies you've told.

NOBODY GETS HURT

is your favorite rationalization.

As you've stated in other entries, you exaggerate
or change stories to make yourself seem more
interesting.

SO, MY LIFE ISN'T
AS DRAMATIC OR
ENTHRALLING AS I
MAKE IT OUT TO BE
SOMETIMES. THAT
DOESN'T MAKE
ANYONE ELSE'S LIFE
ANY WORSE.

IT'S NOT LIKE I'M
KILLING DOGS OR
STEALING MONEY FROM
CHILDREN OR SYMPATHIZING
WITH NAZIS.

But my monster—<u>our</u> monster— has
always known a big secret:
  IF YOU DON'T TELL THE TRUTH,
  YOU'LL NEVER BE ABLE TO TRUST
  THAT YOU'RE WORTHY OF ANYONE'S
  LOVE. In the back of your mind, you'll
  believe that you are not good enough as you are.

After my monster communicated this to me, I took a deep breath, & went inside to tell my husband

ABOUT ALL THE LIES THAT I COULD THINK OF THAT I'D EVER TOLD HIM.

I was SOBBING!

He would probably leave me!

But he did not leave me. He did not love me any less. He said,

IT SEEMS LIKE YOU'RE GOING THROUGH A BIG THING RIGHT NOW. DO YOU WANT ICE CREAM?

I _did_ want ice cream. Now that there was one person who loved me anyway, ice cream felt like something I could & should have.

Slowly, I started telling other people

DIFFICULT TRUTHS

Exactly zero people loved me less. Many of them told me they loved me

EVEN MORE.

You are worthy of love for so many reasons you're not letting yourself believe right now,

& even this letter from me couldn't convince you.

Maybe we all have to go through something like this.

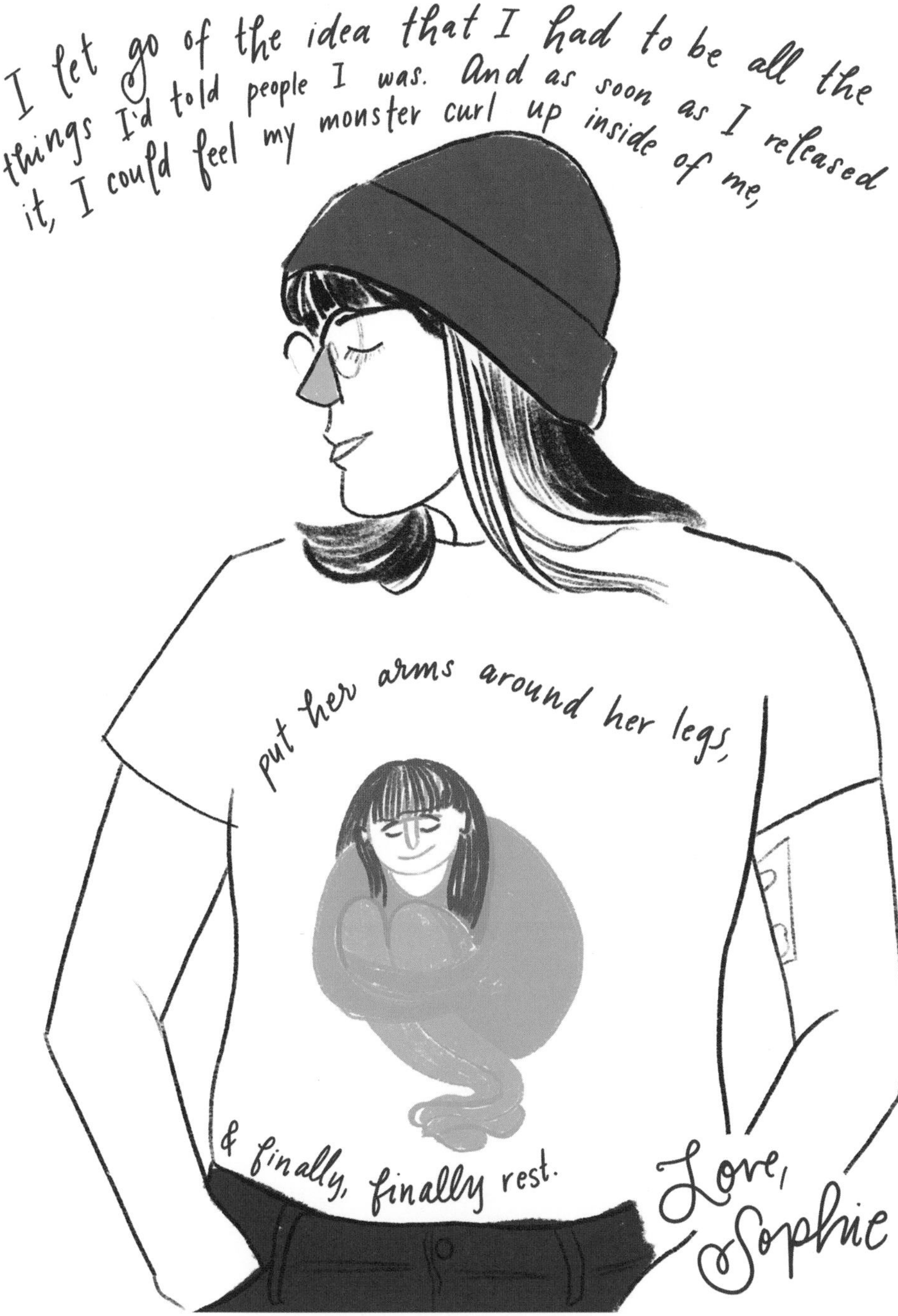
I let go of the idea that I had to be all the things I'd told people I was. And as soon as I released it, I could feel my monster curl up inside of me,
put her arms around her legs,
& finally, finally rest.
Love,
Sophie

chapter
ELEVEN:

Becoming

Dear Sophie,

What do you see yourself becoming?

I mean this in a way that is more abstract than, "Rock star, duh." What are the words that you want to grow into?

I'm curious if what you wanted to become is what I in fact became. Or am I still becoming? Or maybe, are there doors I need to close, so I can find new ones to walk through?

Love,

Sophie

1/8/2002

Dear Diary,

Here are the things I want, in no particular order:

* To go places. Rather, for my future band to go places. I want to make a living playing my music for people, I want them to know all the words to my songs. I want people to look at me in sheer amazement.

Great! I think that will be clarifying.

A few months ago, a girl from high school sent me a message online that said, "I WOKE UP WITH THE LYRICS TO ONE OF YOUR SONGS IN MY HEAD." It was a song I can't remember how to play; you wrote it, back then. This counts a little bit. It's the best I can give you. If it's not enough, maybe Future Sophie will roll up her sleeves & take us both on tour.

For what it's worth, I still really love playing piano. By myself, for myself, to settle my own soul.

211

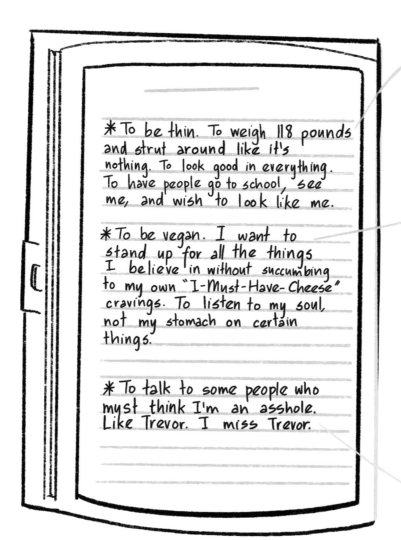

✳ To be thin. To weigh 118 pounds and strut around like it's nothing. To look good in everything. To have people go to school, see me, and wish to look like me.

✳ To be vegan. I want to stand up for all the things I believe in without succumbing to my own "I-Must-Have-Cheese" cravings. To listen to my soul, not my stomach on certain things.

✳ To talk to some people who myst think I'm an asshole. Like Trevor. I miss Trevor.

See pages 56-66. I weigh 181 pounds today. Those are the same numbers (different order), at least!

I am mostly vegan. I still care a lot about this cause. It's kind to animals & it's good for the environment: the end. But I'm also not perfect & I backslide; & we have to choose our battles — there's so much to fight for.

I chose veganism, & I have no space for judgment for people who have chosen other battles. I do believe that whatever you can do & choose to do in the world in order to be the best version of yourself is enough.

(Knowing they're doing a good enough job seems to be the only thing that keeps people going without burning them out.)

See pages 36-41.

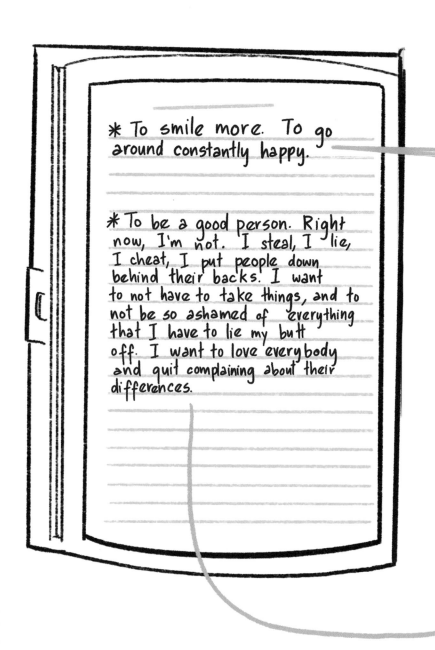

* To smile more. To go around constantly happy.

* To be a good person. Right now, I'm not. I steal, I lie, I cheat, I put people down behind their backs. I want to not have to take things, and to not be so ashamed of everything that I have to lie my butt off. I want to love everybody and quit complaining about their differences.

Ironically, this one makes me sad. I hate that you internalized the whole "smile more" thing. (Most women get told they need to do this. It's a thing.)

Sometimes I'm sad,

sometimes I'm angry,

sometimes I'm contemplative,

sometimes I'm scared.

& sometimes I'm happy.

All of these feelings (& the other 10 trillion feelings I sometimes feel) are so, so valuable!

I don't steal, I don't lie, & I don't say mean things about people behind their backs. But these qualities do not make a person "good."

The idea of good people necessitates that there must also be bad people. I do not believe in bad people.

I think people get hurt & act out of their hurt, & that causes them to behave badly sometimes. I think the worst things humans do come from their most heartbroken child selves, acting out against grownups who hurt them. It is only recently, too, that I started to believe that everyone has the capacity to heal. Maybe I'm wrong, Young Sophie. But I would prefer to believe I'm right.

Instead of being a good person, I strive to be a good animal. That idea comes from a great Barbara Kingsolver essay called "HIGH TIDE IN TUSCON."

Here is what she says:

"IN THE BEST OF TIMES, I HOLD IN MY MIND THE NEED TO CARE FOR THINGS BEYOND THE SELF: POETRY, HUMANITY, GRACE. In OTHER TIMES, WHEN IT SEEMS DIFFICULT MERELY TO SURVIVE & BE HAPPY ABOUT IT, THE CONDITION OF MY THOUGHT TASTES AS SIMPLE AS THIS: LET ME BE A GOOD ANIMAL TODAY."

I'll say this: I do love everybody. I think every-body deserves love, & that love is kind of all humans have going for them.

218

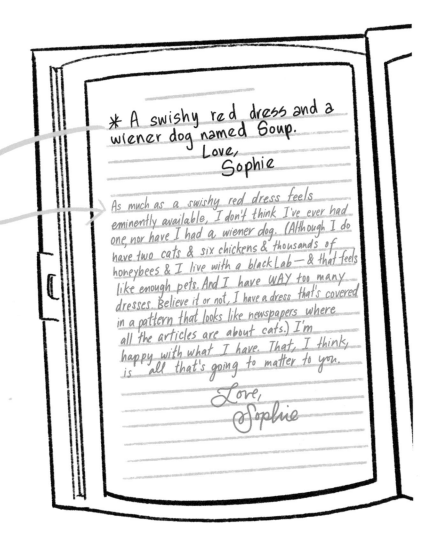

* A swishy red dress and a
wiener dog named Soup.
        Love,
            Sophie

As much as a swishy red dress feels
eminently available, I don't think I've ever had
one, nor have I had a wiener dog. (Although I do
have two cats & six chickens & thousands of
honeybees & I live with a black Lab — & that feels
like enough pets. And I have WAY too many
dresses. Believe it or not, I have a dress that's covered
in a pattern that looks like newspapers where
all the articles are about cats.) I'm
happy with what I have. That, I think,
is all that's going to matter to you.

            Love,
            Sophie

Dear <u>Future</u> Sophie,

I've been writing a lot of letters to a girl we both know pretty well (although I'm a lot closer to her than you are — which is not your fault; you two live way farther apart in the timescape than she & I do). As I write to her, I feel totally wise & grown for the most part. But you know that's not true, huh? You know that I'm being a little bit silly with all this advice & self-assuredness. To be sure, Future Sophie, that's all I know that you know.

I have questions.

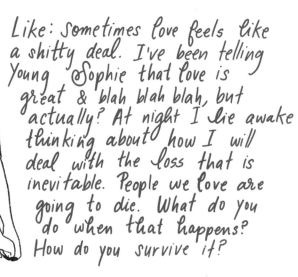

Like: Sometimes love feels like a shitty deal. I've been telling Young Sophie that love is great & blah blah blah, but actually? At night I lie awake thinking about how I will deal with the loss that is inevitable. People we love are going to die. What do you do when that happens? How do you survive it?

Some people I love ♥

What is it like to have a child? Or to not have one? Did I wait too long for that (or for anything else)? What should I be doing more of while I still can, & what am I doing too much of?

Do you regret anything? Do you know anything for sure? Is there a point at which you stop wondering?

If you could, I would love for you to make a list of everything I got wrong, & put gold stars by everything I got right. Take your time, Future Sophie. I'll wait. Love, Sophie

Dear Sophie,

I've been reading your old diaries, looking for deeper meaning or higher purpose. I'm looking for evidence. I want to find my old traumas so that I can decode them & release them & become a better version of myself. I want to find out if I actually, deep down inside, might know or might have always known what really scares me,

& why.

What I notice most
is that you & I are
really different people.
At the end of the
day, this makes me
feel good, for two reasons:

1. When I see you struggling & hurting & striving & trying, I want to take care of you. I feel that way about my students.

They're perfect exactly as they are

& I wish with all my heart I could get them to understand that.

And yet, I often have trouble cutting myself the same slack. But I think I know that Future Sophie will look at me now & have the same compassion for me as I have for you.

So I should try—I should really, really try—to have it for myself.

2. I've learned a lot of things & grown a _lot_. I'm proud.

It took work. It _takes_ work. The work lasts forever & it never stops, so it's nice to take a moment to appreciate where we've been. It inspires me to keep working.

What I didn't find were solutions to my existential puzzles.

There are a lot of semi-OK song lyrics & rhapsodic odes for Rider Strong, & I gained some perspective on issues that I dealt with as a teen & still work through as an adult, but maybe what I've learned is that it's time for me to stop looking back.

I'm grateful to you.
Thank you for sharing this
life with me. But the fact
is the more time I spend
with you, the less time I spend
with **Each Moment Here**.

You can't hold on to anything.
All there is

is now.

& now.

& now.

Love, Sophie

9/30/2001

How often do those fairy tale things come true? I mean, like, when you lie under a tree, and imagine the most perfect thing happening and you destroy yourself over the fact that it will never happen. Perfect things happen to all your friends. They happen to all the people on TV and in the movies. They happen to the rock stars who sing about them on the radio. But never to you. Perfect things never happen to you.

Then, one day, you're doing something, and you realize you don't _need_ perfect things to happen to you. You are happy without them. And you lie awake in bed and feel at one with yourself.

And when you reach that place... only then does something perfect happen to you. A perfect, _perfect_ something. You are sitting somewhere and you take _some_ chance, and all of a sudden you are wrapped in perfection.

I want to recreate the way I've felt for the last couple of weeks. Sadly, I'm unable. It's a blur of emotions.

Perfect things happen to everyone. I have faith in that.

Love, Sophie

Date 9-30-01   4:04 PM   SUNDAY

How often do these fairy tale things come true? I mean, like, when you lie under a tree and imagine the most perfect thing happening and you destroy yourself over the fact that it will never happen. Perfect things happen to all your friends. They happen to all the people on TV and in the movies. They happen to the rock stars who sing about them on the radio. But never to you. Perfect things never happen to you.

Then, one day, you're doing something, and you realise you don't need perfect things to happen to you. You are happy without them. And you lie awake in bed and feel at one with yourself.

And when you reach that place... only then does something perfect happen to you. A perfect, perfect something. You are sitting somewhere and you take some chance, and all of a sudden you are wrapped in perfection.

I want to recreate the way I've felt for the last couple of weeks. Sadly, I'm unable. It's a blur of emotions.

Perfect things happen to everyone. I have faith in that.

♡ S

DP-01

228

2005:

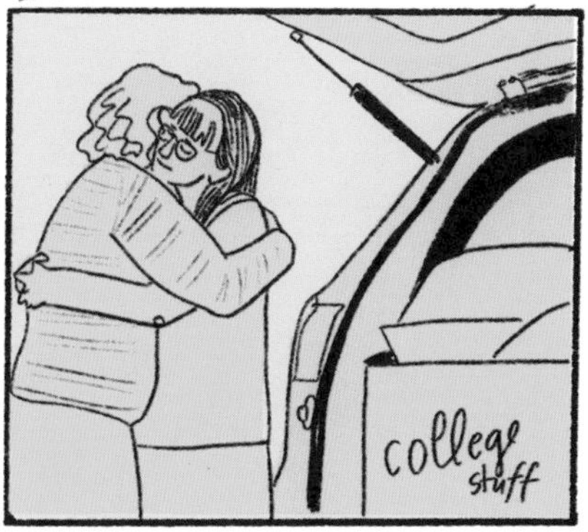
college
stuff

2006:

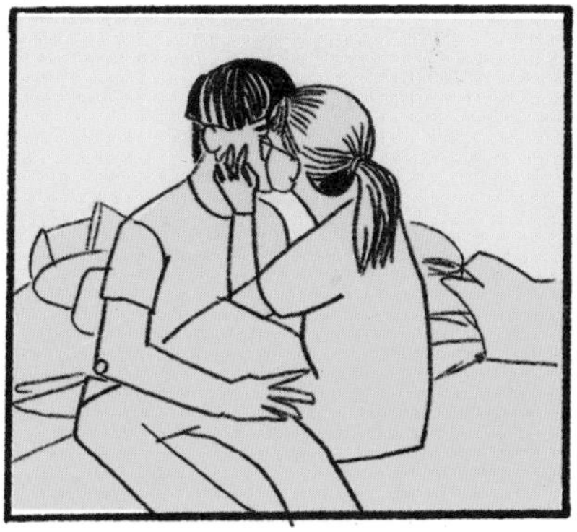

2007:

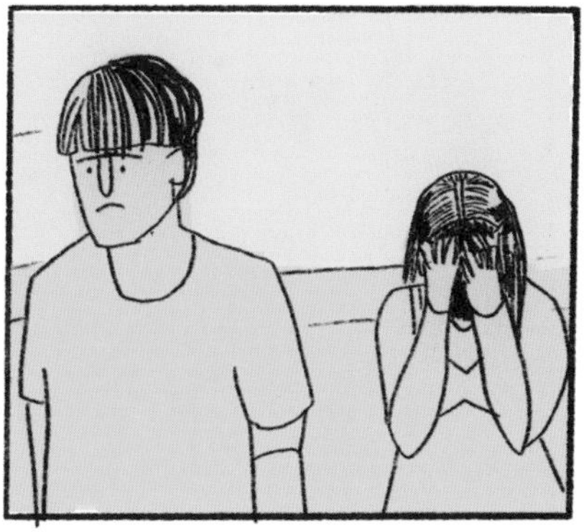

2008:

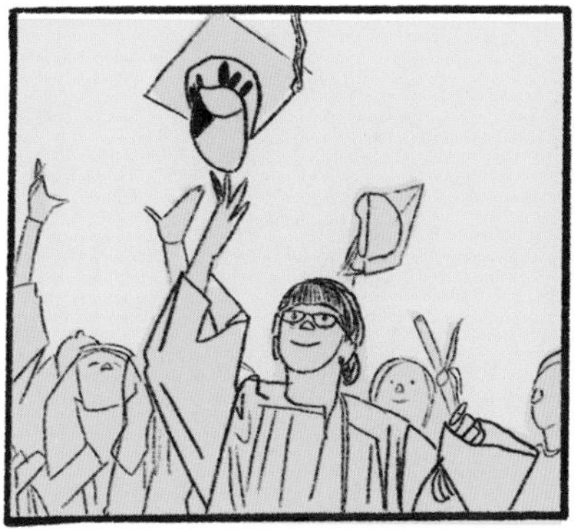

2009:

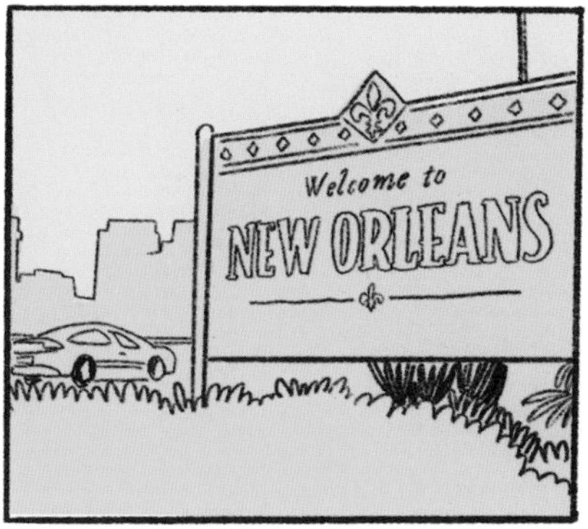
Welcome to
NEW ORLEANS

2010:

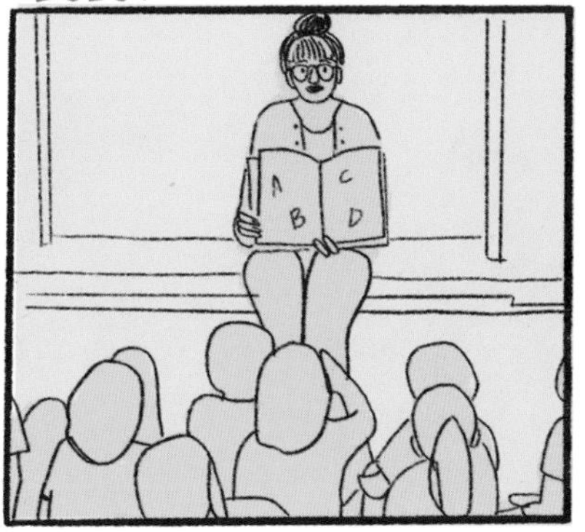
A C
B D

2011:

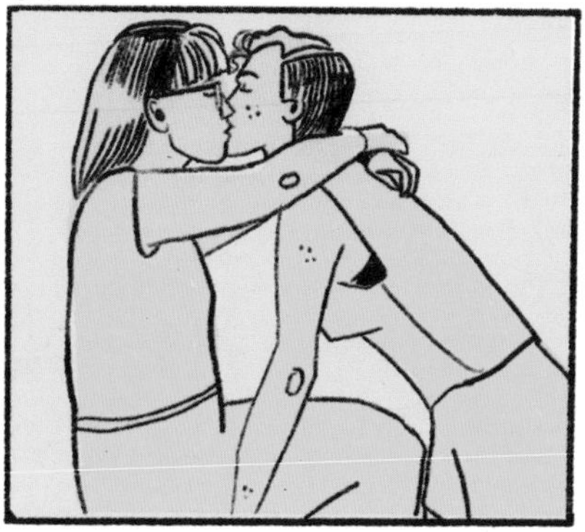

2012:

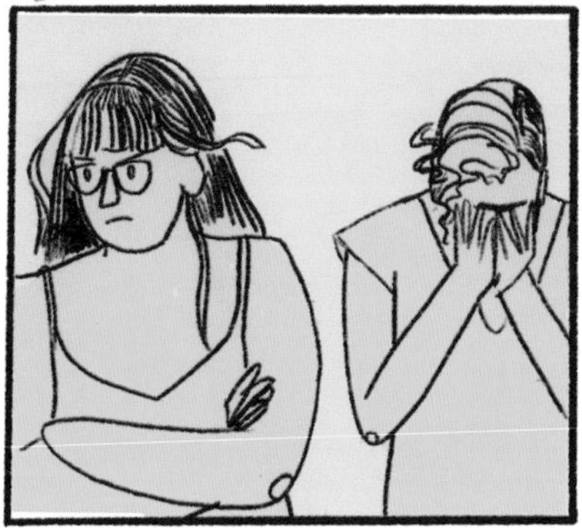

2013:

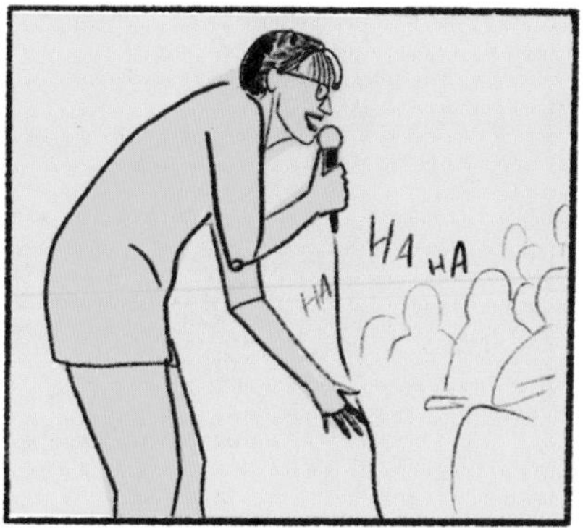
HA
HA HA

2014:

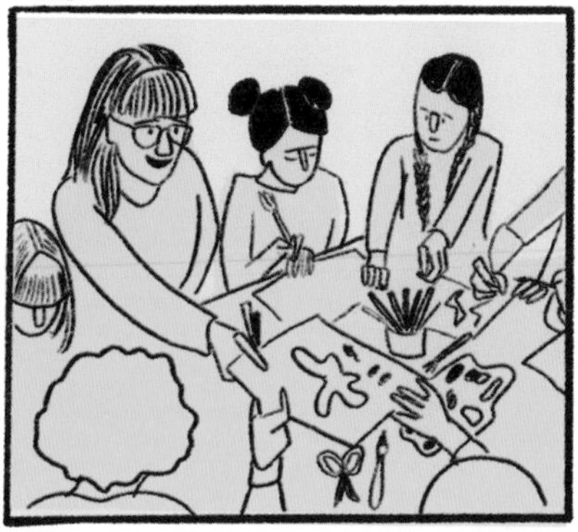

2014:

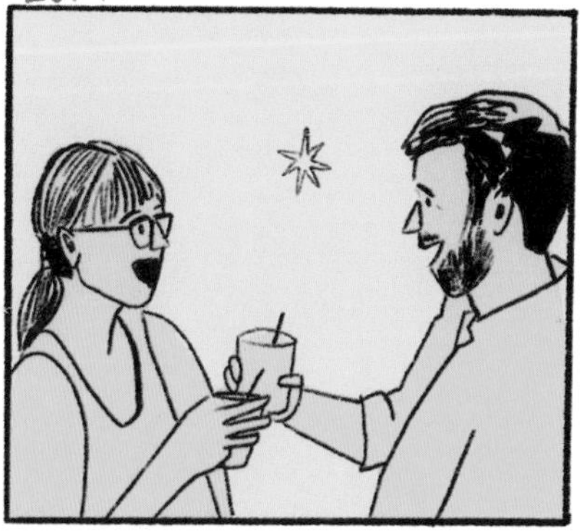

2015:

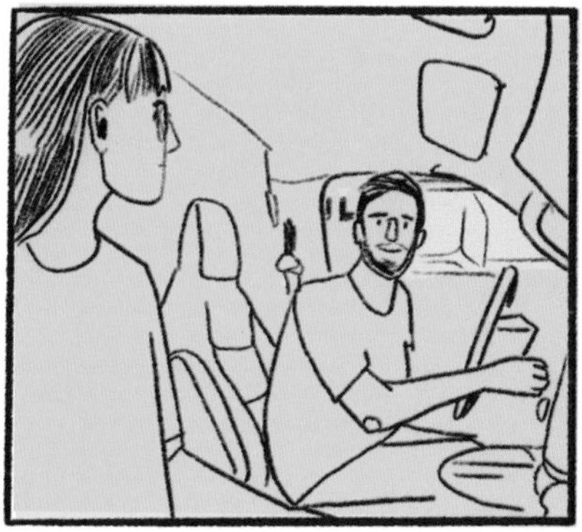

2016:

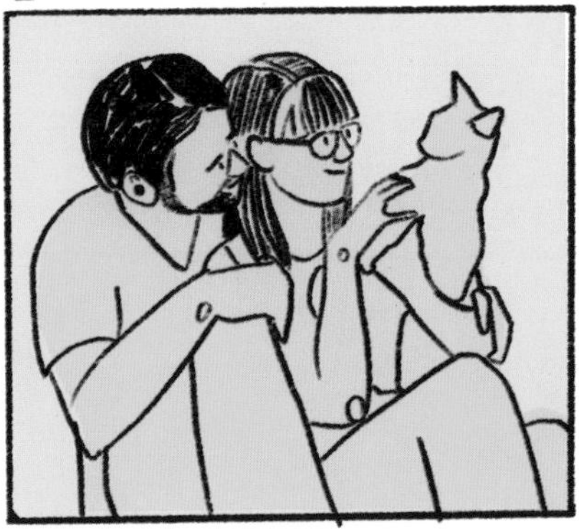

2017:

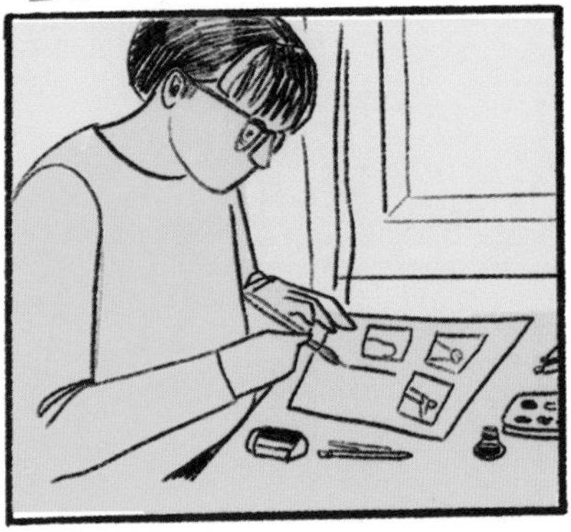

2018:

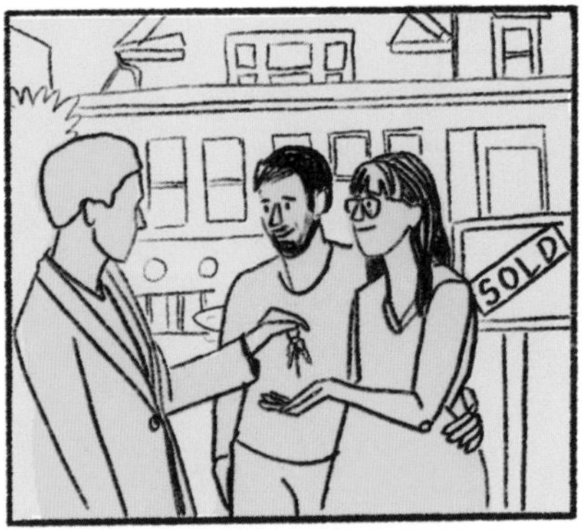
SOLD

2018:

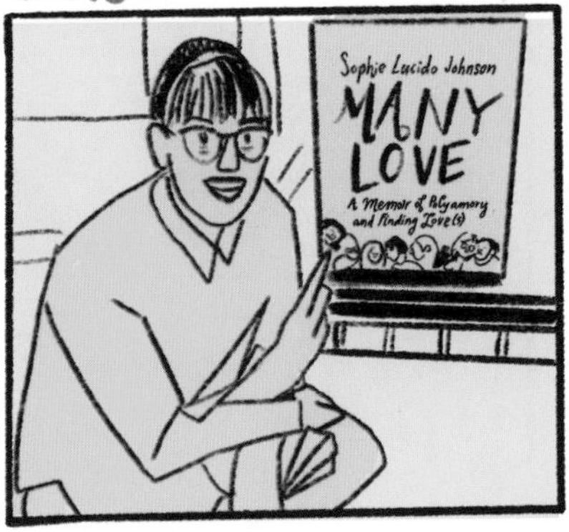
Sophie Lucido Johnson
MANY LOVE
A Memoir of Polyamory and Finding Love(s)

2018:

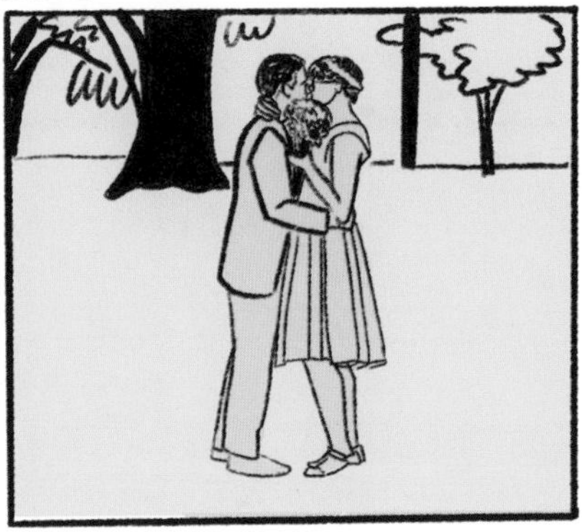

2019:

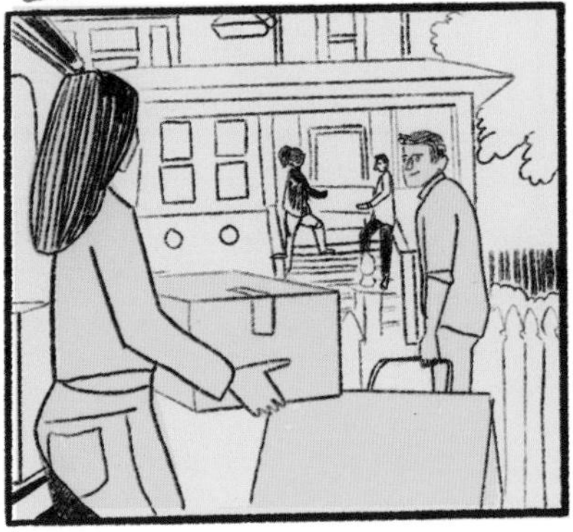

2020:

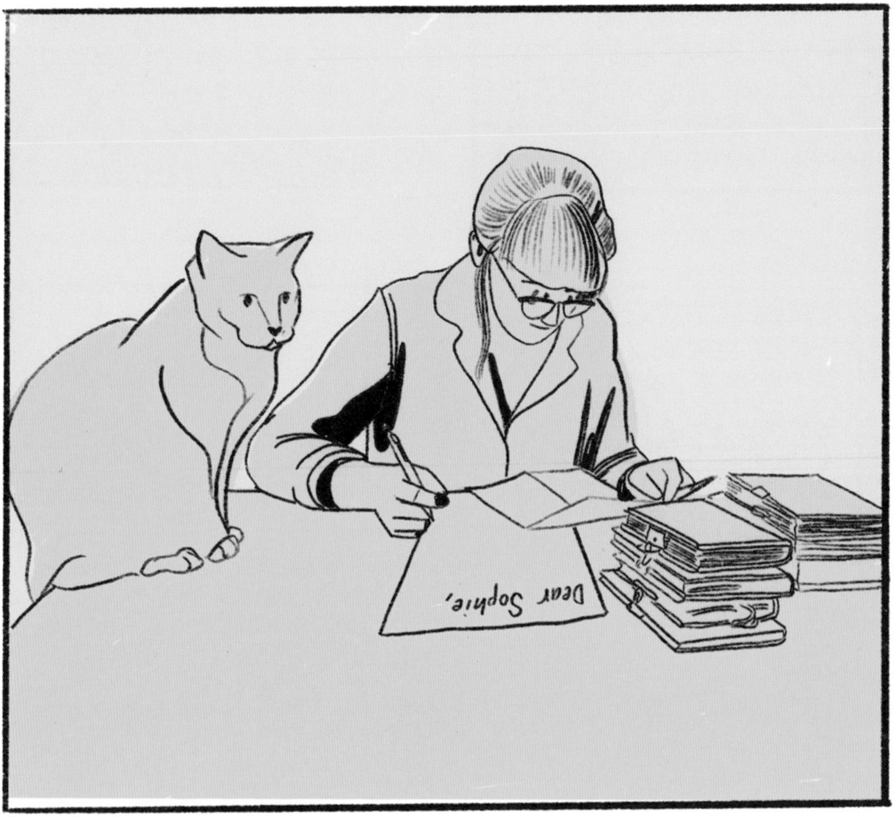
Dear Sophie,

Epilogue

DEAR READER,

IT IS WEIRD TO BE WRITING A BOOK THAT RELIES
SO HEAVILY ON EXISTING IN THE PRESENT MOMENT.
I'M LOOKING BACK AT A PAST THAT'S CONSTANTLY
GROWING AND GROWING AND GROWING. I WRITE THIS
PARTICULAR LETTER IN JANUARY OF 2021, LOOKING
OUT THE WINDOW OF MY CHICAGO HOME AT MORE
THAN A FOOT OF SNOW GLOWING BRIGHT WHITE IN
THE MORNING SUN. IT'S TWELVE DEGREES OUTSIDE.
AS YOU'RE HOLDING THIS BOOK IN YOUR HANDS,

THE WINTER I'M IN NOW IS LONG GONE. EVEN THE
SUMMER I'M LOOKING FORWARD TO HAS COME AND
GONE. YOU'LL KNOW HOW LANGUAGE HAS EVOLVED,
HOW POLICY HAS SHIFTED, HOW OUR CULTURAL
OPINIONS HAVE CHANGED. THERE WILL BE LIVES
THAT HAVE ENDED, AND OTHERS THAT BEGAN.
THERE WILL BE NEW THINGS TO LOVE.

AND THE PRESENT SOPHIE WHO WROTE (AND
IS WRITING) THIS BOOK WILL BE PAST SOPHIE.
SHE'S GONE! SHE'S YOUNG SOPHIE NOW! WHOA!
(I PROMISE I AM NOT ON ANY DRUGS.)

I MENTION THIS BECAUSE <u>EVEN NOW</u>, AS I WRAP THIS
PROJECT UP, THINGS HAVE CHANGED SINCE I WROTE
MY RESPONSES TO YOUNG SOPHIE. FOR EXAMPLE:
I ALREADY HAVE A DIFFERENT RELATIONSHIP WITH
MY BODY THAN I DID WHEN I WROTE THE REST OF
THIS BOOK. I'VE BEEN GOING HARD INTO SOMATIC
THERAPY, TRYING TO DROP INTO MY BODY AND
SLOWLY METABOLIZE MY OWN TRAUMA. A FEW

WEEKS AGO, MY APPENDIX EXPLODED. (I THINK
THESE THINGS ARE RELATED.) MY BODY-SPECIFIC
NEW YEAR'S RESOLUTION WAS TO NOT COUNT
CALORIES AND NOT WEIGH MYSELF AT ALL. I'VE
BEEN PLAYING THE PIANO AND SINGING MORE—
EVEN WHEN PEOPLE ARE HOME, SOMETIMES. I
STILL HAVEN'T CUT MYSELF—IT'S THE LONGEST
NOT-CUTTING STREAK I'VE HAD SINCE I WAS SIXTEEN.
A LOT OF THESE CHANGES (IF NOT ALL) HAVE COME
ABOUT <u>BECAUSE</u> I WROTE THE LETTERS IN THIS
BOOK. IT'S A BIT SHAMEFUL TO TAKE A LONG, HARD
LOOK AT YOUR CHILD SELF AND BE LIKE, "YEAH, I
STILL THINK I'M FAT AND I STILL THINK THAT'S A
PROBLEM AND I SPEND A LOT OF TIME AND MONEY
ON THAT." I WANT TO DO RIGHT BY YOUNG SOPHIE,
FUTURE SOPHIE, AND ALL THE PEOPLE (WHO ARE
PROBABLY NOT NAMED SOPHIE, BUT THERE MAY BE
A FEW OTHER SOPHIES OUT THERE) WHO MIGHT
BE AFFECTED BY MY SELF-PERCEPTION.

I'VE WALKED TO LAKE MICHIGAN ALMOST EVERY DAY IN JANUARY. THIS RITUAL IS KEEPING ME WHOLE. SO MANY HUMANS BEFORE ME HAVE UNDERSTOOD THE WISDOM OF WATER. LOOKING AT WATER FEELS LIKE RINGING ONE OF THOSE SOFT, MEDITATIVE CHIMES THEY HAVE IN YOGA STUDIOS.

YESTERDAY, THE LAKE WAS BOUNDED BY HILLS OF ICE. WAVES HAD SPLASHED UP AND OVER THE GUARD RAILS ONTO THE ROAD, ENCASING THE NEAREST PARKED CARS IN INCH-DEEP ICE. THERE WERE SNOWBANKS AND ICICLES, AND TRULY I FELT LIKE I WAS ON A POSTAPOCALYPTIC BEACH ON A MOON IN A FANTASY NOVEL. THE DAY BEFORE, THERE HAD BEEN LITTLE MOUNDS OF SNOW AND SLIPPERY SURFACES NEAR THE SHORE, WITH GENTLE, SHUDDERING WAVES SMOOTHING OUT THE ROCKS. THE WEEK BEFORE WE'D HAD SUN, AND YOU COULD HAVE BEEN FORGIVEN FOR LOOKING OUT AT THE BRIGHT BLUE WATER AND THINKING IT WAS SUMMER. STANDING IN THE SAME SPOT ON MY

WALK EVERY DAY, I NEVER SEE ANYTHING THAT FEELS LIKE IT'S STAYED THE SAME. THE WATER GENTLY GETS ITS MESSAGE ACROSS: "CHANGE IS ALL THERE IS. THERE IS NOTHING ELSE."

SO, READER, I'M NOT SURE <u>WHAT</u> HAS CHANGED BETWEEN YOUR PAST AND YOUR NOW—THE MOMENT AND SITUATION YOU'RE CURRENTLY IN—BUT I KNOW THAT THINGS HAVE CHANGED. IF YOU'RE IN A PLACE IN YOUR LIFE WHERE YOU FEEL STUCK, I WANT YOU TO KNOW THAT THINGS WILL CONTINUE TO CHANGE.

LOVE,
SOPHIE

My Holy Books Shelf

MY IDEAS AND REVELATIONS ARE INFORMED
ENORMOUSLY IF NOT ENTIRELY BY MY TEACHERS.
A HUGE NUMBER OF THOSE TEACHERS DON'T KNOW
ME PERSONALLY BUT HAVE WRITTEN BOOKS THAT I
RETURN TO OVER AND OVER AGAIN. I KEEP THOSE
BOOKS ON A SPECIAL, HIGH-UP SHELF JUST BEHIND
MY DESK. IT IS IMPORTANT TO GIVE CREDIT TO THEM
HERE, AND TO HUMBLY ENTREAT YOU TO READ THEM.
I BELIEVE WITH MY WHOLE HEART THAT IF EVERYONE
READ EVERY BOOK ON MY HOLY BOOKS SHELF, THE
WORLD WOULD BE A RADICALLY BETTER PLACE.

MY BIG THREE

My
Grandmother's
Hands
Racialized Trauma and the Pathway to
Mending Our Hearts and Bodies
RESMAA MENAKEM
MSW, LICSW, SEP

EMER
GEAT
STRA
TEGY

SHAPING CHANGE, CHANGING WORLDS
adrienne maree brown

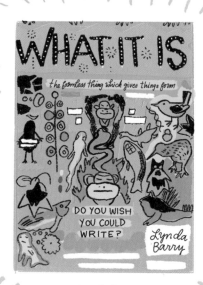

WHAT·IT·IS
the formless thing which gives things form

DO YOU WISH
YOU COULD
WRITE?

Lynda
Barry

Additional Faves:

- <u>Intuitive Eating: A Revolutionary Program That Works</u>, Evelyn Tribole & Elyse Resch

- <u>Radical Honesty</u>, Brad Blanton

- <u>Pleasure Activism: The Politics of Feeling Good</u>, adrienne maree brown

- <u>Go Tell It on the Mountain</u>, James Baldwin

- <u>How to Do Nothing: Resisting the Attention Economy</u>, Jenny Odell

- <u>Daring Greatly: How the Courage to Be Vulnerable Transforms the Way We Live, Love, Parent, and Lead</u>, Brené Brown

- <u>All About Love: New Visions</u>, bell hooks

- <u>I'm in Charge of Celebrations</u>, Byrd Baylor

- <u>Pedagogy of the Oppressed</u>, Paulo Freire

- <u>The Selected Works of Audre Lorde</u>, Audre Lorde

- <u>Heavy: An American Memoir</u>, Kiese Laymon

- <u>What It's Like to Be a Bird: From Flying to Nesting, Eating to Singing—What Birds Are Doing, and Why</u>, David Sibley

- <u>Braiding Sweetgrass: Indigenous Wisdom, Scientific Knowledge, and the Teachings of Plants</u>, Robin Wall Kimmerer

- <u>How to Be an Antiracist</u>, Ibram X. Kendi

- <u>Citizen: An American Lyric</u>, Claudia Rankine

- <u>The Shock Doctrine: The Rise of Disaster Capitalism</u>, Naomi Klein

- <u>Bad Feminist: Essays</u>, Roxane Gay

- <u>Veganomicon</u>, Isa Chandra Moskowitz

- <u>Big Magic: Creative Living Beyond Fear</u>, Elizabeth Gilbert

- <u>Shrill: Notes from a Loud Woman</u>, Lindy West

- <u>How We Show Up: Reclaiming Family, Friendship, and Community</u>, Mia Birdsong

- <u>The Polyamorists Next Door: Inside Multiple Partner Relationships and Families</u>, Elisabeth Sheff

Gratitude:

IT IS WILD TO ME THAT WHEN I WRITE A BOOK
IT'S ONLY MY NAME THAT GOES ON THE FRONT OF
IT. EVEN THIS BOOK, WHICH IS FILLED WITH THE
WORD "SOPHIE," IS NOT SOMETHING THAT BELONGS
TO ME, EVEN A LITTLE BIT. MACKENZIE BRADY
WATSON, AEMILIA PHILLIPS, AND THE TEAM AT
HARPERONE—ESPECIALLY KATHRYN HAMILTON
AND CHANTAL TOM— SHOULD ALSO HAVE THEIR
NAMES ON THE COVER. IT IS AS MUCH THEIR WORK
AS IT IS MINE.

JILL RIDDELL AND RAGHAV RAO AND THE OFFICE OF MODERN COMPOSITION ARE RESPONSIBLE FOR THE VERY IMPORTANT CONFETTI PARTIES THAT HAPPENED THROUGHOUT THIS PROCESS. THIS IS A SEMI-VAPID WAY OF DISGUISING A GENUINELY DEEP THANK-YOU: THERE IS NOTHING IN MY WRITING LIFE THAT WOULD HAPPEN WITHOUT THE OMC.

MY FAMILY, GIVEN AND CHOSEN, HAS BEEN GENEROUS WITH THEIR TIME, THEIR PATIENCE, THEIR LOVE, AND THEIR GENTLE MOTIVATION WHILE I SAID ONE HUNDRED TRILLION TIMES: "OH MY GOD, IT IS SO HARD TO WRITE A GRAPHIC NOVEL. WHY DID I THINK I COULD DO THIS? I REGRET ALL MY CHOICES." TO NAME A FEW (IN ALPHABETICAL ORDER BECAUSE THERE'S NO APPROPRIATE ORDER): ALBERT, AMINISHA, ANN, ARI, BEN, BEN, BOB, BRETT, CAROL, DAD, DAMIEN, DAN, DOROTHEA, DYLAN, ERIN, GRANDMAS, GRANDPAS, HANNAH, JEN, JESS, JESSE, JILL, JOE, KIM, MARY, MARY-ELLEN, MIA, MOM, NOAH, OSCAR, PARIS, PEGGY, RACHEL,

ROBERT, RUBY, SAM, SAMMI, STEPHEN, SUE, VINCENT. THANKS TOO TO THOSE I'VE ABSENTMINDEDLY FORGOTTEN.

THANK YOU TO BETHANY, WHO IS IN HER OWN CATEGORY. YOU HAVE LISTENED TO ME COMPLAIN PROBABLY THE MOST OUT OF EVERYONE. I DON'T KNOW HOW TO EXPLAIN OUR LOVE TO PEOPLE, BUT WHOA DO I EVER LOVE AND APPRECIATE YOU.

AND TO ALEXIS, WHO DID AN ENORMOUS AMOUNT OF LISTENING, ENCOURAGING, REVIEWING, AND ACCEPTING. ALEXIS, THANKS FOR THOSE THINGS, AND FOR LETTING ME WRITE ABOUT YOU, AND FOR BEING FUN TO DRAW.

TREVOR, JOE, ELI, MOM, WEIRD AL, RIDER STRONG, AND MANY, MANY HUMANS WHOSE NAMES HAVE BEEN CHANGED: THANKS SO MUCH FOR LETTING ME TELL MY ONE-SIDED VERSION OF A FRACTION OF THE STORY OF OUR LIVES TOGETHER.

THANKS TO EACH AND EVERY ONE OF MY STUDENTS,
PAST, PRESENT, AND FUTURE. YOU ARE MY
FAVORITE LIVING PEOPLE. THANK YOU FOR HELPING
TO FIX THE EARTH WE BROKE.

PENULTIMATELY (I JUST <u>LOVE</u> THE WORD
"PENULTIMATELY" AND USE IT AS OFTEN AS
POSSIBLE, I'M AFRAID): I HAVE THREE PARTNERS.
WHEN A PERSON IS WORKING ON A BOOK, IT
REQUIRES MORE FROM ONE'S PARTNERS THAN AN
ACKNOWLEDGMENTS SECTION COULD EVER HOLD.
BOB, THE HOURS WE HAVE SPENT PROCESSING
OUR LIVES HAVE MADE ME A BETTER PERSON, AND
YOU ARE ALSO A GENIUS. KAT, I ADMIRE YOUR
DILIGENCE, YOUR HUMOR, YOUR MORAL COMPASS,
YOUR GRASP OF THE WRITTEN WORD, AND YOUR
BEAUTIFUL SMILE. LUKE, I WISH EVERYONE ON
EARTH KNEW YOU AND COULD BE LOVED BY YOU,
BECAUSE YOU ARE THE ANTIDOTE TO ALL THINGS,
AND YOU MAKE SUCH A HEALING CUP OF TEA.

I LOVE YOU AND AM GRATEFUL FOR YOU ALL SO, SO, SO INCREDIBLY MUCH. TIMES INFINITY, TIMES A MILLION, FOREVER.

TO YOU, READER, IF YOU'VE MADE IT THIS FAR: YOUR TIME IS AN INCREDIBLE GIFT. I AM HUMBLED AND HONORED THAT YOU'VE GIVEN IT TO ME AND TO THESE PAGES. THANK YOU.